I DON'T GOT THIS

I DON'T GOT THIS

ADVENTURES IN SCHIZOPHRENIA AND ALCOHOLISM

EMILY JOURNEY

Copyright © 2021 by Emily Journey
All rights reserved.

No part of this book may be reproduced in any form or by any electronic or mechanical means, including information storage and retrieval systems, without written permission from the author, except for the use of brief quotations in a book review.

Excerpts from PIPPI LONGSTOCKING by Astrid Lindgren, translated by Florence Lamborn, translation copyright 1950, renewed © 1978 by Penguin Random House LLC. Used by permission of Viking Children's Books, an imprint of Penguin Young Readers Group, a division of Penguin Random House LLC. All rights reserved.

Library of Congress Cataloging-in Publication Data is available.

ISBN 978-1-7372781-0-8 (paperback)
ISBN 978-1-7372781-1-5 (ebook)

Cover design and chapter illustrations by Katie Zupan
Cover illustration by Riley Samels

Visit https://idontgotthisbook.com for author notes and bonus content for readers.

© Sunnyslope Press

To Barbara and Rachel

"Oh, what will happen? Oh, I'm so nervous. What if I can't behave myself?"

"Of course you can," said Annika.

"Don't you be too certain about that," said Pippi. "You can be sure I'll try, but I have noticed several times that people don't think I know how to behave even when I'm trying as hard as I can."

— Pippi Longstocking[1]

SWAT

In November 2014 my mom, Chlotene Tubbs, set fire to her neighbor's front door in the hallway of the senior apartment complex where she lived alone. She was seventy-four.

I had just started my own business that was shakily gaining steam. I was in the middle of a disintegrating marriage that would end in my third divorce. I'd had three spinal surgeries in the past six years. And I had quit drinking after five years of getting drunk almost every day. I was forty-four.

Chlotene's apartment was in Westerville, a suburb of Columbus, Ohio. She set fire to the door in November. More precisely, she set fire to a (very flammable) festive straw scarecrow hanging on the door—one of those decorations you might pick up in a drugstore when you went to get deodorant or toilet paper or something.

She called me the next day to tell me the police had come. She gave me a number, and I called the detective assigned to her case. We agreed I'd bring her in the next day to get her mugshot and fingerprints taken.

When we were down at the station, the detective let me know that because my mother's charge involved arson, he would have to go downtown to the county prosecutor's office and present the report in person.

"OK," I said. I was hustling to get her a psychiatric evaluation. I couldn't really think beyond the next few days, even though I knew arson was a felony. At the time, Chlotene was a kindly looking white lady who looked older than her seventy-four years, and maybe that's why he told us we were free to go once she'd been booked, without any further instructions about where she needed to go next or what she needed to do. I don't know.

The next time I heard from the police was a few days later when an eight-man SWAT team in full tactical gear showed up at Chlotene's door to haul her in. She'd been charged with a first-degree felony. But she wasn't at home.

Chlotene had checked herself into the psychiatric ward of a local hospital on the basis of the evaluation I had organized a few days earlier.

As we sat in the psychiatrist's office on the day she was hospitalized, the doctor asked Chlotene a series of questions, then turned to me and said, "I'm going to recommend immediate hospitalization. She's set a fire, and it's clear she is a danger to others."

For the first time in my life, I was hearing from a licensed psychiatrist that my mother had a mental illness so severe that she needed medical attention. *Screw it!* Not just medical attention—she needed round-the-clock hospital care.

I had lived my entire life with a mother who was sick but

undiagnosed and untreated. I had begun to suspect she had schizophrenia nearly twenty years earlier, when I was finishing my master's degree in social work. When I was in my late twenties, I started testing the words "My mom has schizophrenia" out loud.

But even when I said it to someone, I would hear some version of the question, "How do you know?"

Has she seen a doctor?
What kind of medication is she taking?
Oh, she doesn't take medication?
Where does she live? On her own? Not in a . . . facility? (You know, for those *kinds of people?)*

Or I might get nothing more than a questioning look, especially from people who knew her. After all, they saw her as a functioning person. A person who'd raised me on her own as a single mother. A person who held down jobs and lived in an apartment. Their preexisting image of a schizophrenic as an actively psychotic homeless man didn't fit.

Technically, once the doctor recommended hospitalization, Chlotene was the one who had to check herself in. I couldn't "commit" her because she wasn't deemed an imminent violent threat. But she put up precious little resistance to admitting herself to the hospital. An anticlimactic end, really, to decades of avoiding doctors and diagnoses and getting any help.

She did worry aloud that she would miss the appointment she'd made with the cable guy.

"Don't worry," I told her. "I'll let the cable guy in."

That's how it happened that on a cold, gray day in November, about ten days after setting the fire, Chlotene was hospitalized for a psychotic break, and I was headed to her new apartment. Her move to a new senior-living apartment complex a few miles from where she'd set the fire had already been planned, and the movers had transferred her belongings just a couple of days earlier.

I unlocked the door and stepped inside. The movers had unpacked most of her meager possessions, although she had five or six boxes left to sort through. Her furniture was arranged in the living room—her desk hugging the wall on one side of the room, a small table on the other side, the television, and her couch across from it.

As soon as I sat down, I heard a banging knock at the door. I opened it to see an officer leaning against the door jamb, his face inches from mine. A second officer stood just to his left.

Along with them, six other SWAT-team cops lined the walls of the hallway. They were all wearing black bulletproof vests, black bulletproof helmets, and black rifles slung across their shoulders.

The building manager also showed up. He was deaf, so along with him came his sign language interpreter. Altogether, I was staring at ten people when I opened the door.

The officer nearest to my face barked at me, "Do you own a green Volkswagen Passat?" just as the second officer barked, "Are you Chlotene Tubbs?"

Confused, I said no. Didn't they have a physical description of Chlotene? She was thirty years older than me, three inches shorter, and maybe eighty pounds heavier. She had very short graying hair, while I had shoulder-length auburn hair.

But before I could process my confusion over how they could confuse me with my mother, the two officers in front pushed their heads into the doorway, alongside them the building manager and his interpreter.

The sign language interpreter began to sign and speak the words to the building manager, echoing the aggression in the faces of the SWAT-team cops. I didn't immediately realize she was there to interpret.

I shifted into a cool, calm character. I'd had to find this mode so many times throughout my life to handle one crazy situation after another. I slipped into it like a second skin.

"Chlotene's my mom. I'm her daughter. I'm here waiting for the cable company," I said in a low-pitched, confident voice.

"Where is she?" one of them said, and the sign-language interpreter echoed his angry bark with her gestures. She, too, said, "Where is she?"

"She's at Dublin Springs Hospital," I said. Then I turned to the interpreter and said it again.

"Why is she in the hospital?" asked the officer leaning against the door jamb.

"She has schizophrenia and she's getting treatment," I said.

Then the interpreter repeated the question. "Why is she in the hospital?"

"She has schizophrenia and she's getting treatment," I repeated to the interpreter.

She turned and shot me a look of exasperation. It registered with me that she hadn't been talking to me at all. She was totally focused on her job of interpretation, and I could stop answering the same question twice.

"We have a warrant for her arrest," the officer in front of me said.

"OK," I said.

As they asked me more questions, the building manager was simultaneously asking me, "What happened? Why are these people here for your mom?" His sign language interpreter was peppering in his questions while they both signed furiously, adding to the general sense of commotion.

"Well, she was paranoid," I explained. "She's getting treatment in the hospital. She's stable now," I added, suddenly realizing I should try to cover for Chlotene to minimize the possibility that she would lose her new apartment. "She's getting medication."

"Is she going to do it again?" the manager asked.

"No, no, no, this was a breakdown. She wasn't taking her medication," I said, leaving out the fact that she wasn't taking her medication because up until three days before, she hadn't had a psychiatrist since the mid-1960s. He didn't have to know that part.

The SWAT team reinserted themselves. "We're going to the hospital to pick her up," one of them said accusingly, as though I might be hiding something.

"OK," I said. What could I be hiding? As if I was going to do anything to stop a SWAT team wearing their rifles like beauty pageant sashes across their chests.

Everyone filed out, and the door shut.

I took a breath, dug out my cell phone, and called the hospital.

"Hello?"

"Hi," I said. "I know you're not able to give out any patient information, but my mom was just admitted a couple of days ago."

"I'm not able to confirm or deny that anyone is a patient here, ma'am," the receptionist said. "Our policy is to protect patient privacy," she added, wearily preempting any argument.

"Right, I know," I said, plunging ahead. "But I need to let you know . . . there's an eight-man SWAT team on their way to you to pick her up."

"OK, ma'am," she said in her world-weary voice. She sounded used to all sorts of people showing up at the front desk, and I was having trouble communicating why this time might be different.

The beauty pageant sash rifles. The helmets. The barking questions.

"I need you to take down my name and number and give them to your director as soon as we hang up," I said, my voice clear and steady: a fighter pilot radioing troops on the ground. "Because she is going to want to call me. I know you can't confirm or deny anything, but have her call me. I am sitting right by my phone."

The drive from my mother's apartment building to the hospital had taken me thirty-five minutes the last time I'd done it. I got a call in fifteen.

"They're here."

PART I

. . . But the ringmaster didn't laugh. He turned toward an attendant in a red uniform and made a sign to him to go and stop the horse.

"Is this act already over," asked Pippi in a disappointed tone, "just when we were having so much fun?"

"Horrible child!" hissed the ringmaster between his teeth. "Get out of here!"

Pippi looked at him sadly. "Why are you mad at me?" she asked. "What's the matter? I thought we were here to have fun."[1]

1

Things My Mother Thought Were Happening, 1970–2014

HER ROOMMATE WAS OPENING her mail. Every roommate was opening her mail.

———

Her neighbors had somehow gotten a key to her apartment and were letting themselves in to hack into her email when she wasn't home.

———

Her coworkers used her computer when she wasn't around and left stuff there to get her in trouble.

———

Her next-door neighbor was running a prostitution ring. Her granddaughters were somehow roped into the prostitution ring. The cops were her neighbor's "biggest clients." They confirmed this suspicion when they stopped coming to her apartment complex after the second time she called them.

———

She was related to just about everyone she met—including the Hostess delivery truck driver that her son John happened to park next to when he took her to the dentist one day. And she ran up to the driver to tell him so.

———

She met Osama Bin Laden in a nursing home where she worked. He had "tall man's syndrome," so when he wore a turban on his head, it grazed the ceiling.

———

She had met several famous criminals. She had dated Richard Speck before I was born. Richard Speck, the man who, according to his Wikipedia page, "systematically raped one and tortured and murdered eight student nurses from South Chicago Community Hospital on the night of July 13 into the early morning hours of July 14, 1966."

(They didn't have Wikipedia back then.)

———

A woman in our church was trying to seduce the pastor. So was a second woman, who "stuck her ass in the air to get the pastor's attention." And she ran up to the women to tell them so.

When I was twelve years old and preparing for my baptism at our church, I was "trying to get raped." Or "trying to have sex."

On the third floor, at one end of her apartment building, she could hear conversations on the first floor at the other end of the building. "The walls are thin," she'd say by way of explanation.
 It didn't matter that that was impossible.

Things That I Thought Were Normal, 1970–1979

My mother told me that she had shown up at the airport one day, walked up to a counter, and told the agent how much money she had and that she wanted a ticket to someplace warm. The agent suggested Phoenix.

 (When I was an adult, I found out that this story was true, but that she had left out the fact that she had given birth and placed a baby—my half-sister Michelle—up for adoption two weeks before she made that trip to the airport. Five months later, she was pregnant with me.)

When I was four, Chlotene left me with a family in our apartment complex who looked after me. They had a mom and a dad, which I know now was unusual among the families who lived in our complex. And they had two boys, four and twelve. The older boy regularly egged the younger one on until he beat me up. Whenever the parents happened to see us, they laughed.

I looked for a hiding place in every place we ever lived in case it was ever broken into while I was home alone. A place I could go where the intruders wouldn't be able to find me.

People jiggled our front doorknob regularly. Once I opened the front door on a group of teenagers that were trying to pick the lock. They ran away.

When I was growing up, my hiding place was usually under the kitchen sink. We never had anything under there when I was kid, so I could fit. I used to practice tucking myself into the cabinet, staying silent in the dark. "Emily?" my mom would call, and I'd come rolling out from beneath the sink.

When I got too big for the sink, I shifted my hiding place to disguised arrangements of dirty laundry in a closet. I have a hiding place in my house now, but I'm not going to write it here. Then it wouldn't be hidden.

In Phoenix in the 1970s, I liked to pick up half-smoked cigarettes off the ground in the parking lot, take them back to the apartment, light them on the stove, and try to smoke them.

I played in the back of unlocked cars in the parking lot of the apartment complexes where we lived. I was good about not stealing the change I found.

I didn't go to the dentist until I was fifteen. At my first visit, the dentist didn't believe I'd never been to a dentist before. I think he became convinced after he found sixteen cavities.

Even though I got decent grades, I had to forge my mom's signature on my report card because she couldn't be bothered to take a look. Other kids got so stressed out whenever report cards came out. My mother never cared. Why did their parents care so much?

One summer day, when I was about five years old, Chlotene left me at a daycare center somewhere in Phoenix, and she didn't come back for me.

I played all day. Then, one by one, the other kids went home. I watched as their parents came to get them, looking up at the door every time it opened. Moms came in mostly, a few smiling, many tired and stern. They collected their children and walked them out, hand in hand.

And then it was just me and a couple of the daycare workers who stayed with me. They turned out the lights on the daycare center and walked me into the main office. They had a cot in there.

I heard them talking about how they could not get ahold of my mother; she wasn't answering the phone number she gave them. They kept asking me if I knew when my mom was going to come to pick me up.

"I don't know," I said. Then I asked, "Can I live with you? Then we could just go home now. We wouldn't have to wait for my mom."

One of the women furrowed her brow. "Let's just see if we can find her," she answered.

Eventually Chlotene arrived. It was dark in the office and felt very late. I had fallen asleep on the cot.

I didn't see a confrontation, but I do know that I never went back there. In any case, even if she hadn't turned up hours late to pick me up, I probably wouldn't have been back very much. Chlotene usually couldn't afford to pay for childcare.

She did say she thought that the daycare was open twenty-four hours a day. She was constantly misinterpreting the world around her, and this daycare was no exception. She needed a daycare with extended hours, so her brain told her she had found one.

"Let's go," she said as I got my shoes on and stumbled outside with her. I felt a tinge of disappointment. Her showing up ruined the plan I'd cooked up to be adopted by a nice family. None of the other parents *forgot* that the daycare wasn't twenty-four hours. None of the other parents were like this. Why was she?

We headed outside, where it was dusk. Normally, we took the bus. But this evening she picked me up in a white van.

Where did she get the white van? As a five-year-old, I didn't wonder about it, but I do now. I really don't know. It's not likely that she even had a driver's license. She probably didn't even have the title. Odds are she handed over a wad of cash from her tax refund in exchange for the keys. And that was that.

I don't remember what happened to this particular white van, but I do remember her abandoning a different car later on in my childhood. She couldn't afford to put gas in it, so she parked it and walked away.

This white van was the kind a painter or a plumber would have, so it only had one seat—the driver's seat. The rest was an empty, windowless cavern, with scratches all over the interior white paint.

I climbed in and tried to settle myself on the corrugated metal floor, right behind my mom's seat. We pulled out of the daycare parking lot. The waves in the metal floor made it impossible to find a position I could sit in. So I stood up and started walking around in the back.

"Sit down!" Chlotene shouted as we picked up speed. I pretended to be a monkey, finding hand and foot holds as the force of the van picking up speed began to push me back, away from the driver's seat.

Then, the doors in the back of the van flew open. The light of a bright streetlamp flooded into the back of the dark van.

As I tumbled toward the open doors, I got a glimpse of the black top. It looked liquid, a rapid black river with a steady bright yellow line that I could follow to a place far away from here. Somewhere—anywhere—else.

I can just jump out, I thought before my scrawny five-year-old hand gripped a ridge in the van wall to steady myself.

Chlotene pulled to the side of the road. I watched her shut the doors. The back of the windowless van instantly went dark. We continued on, but after a few more minutes, a cop pulled Chlotene over. Expired tags.

When my own daughters were little, we would go to the public library almost every day. I was in my early twenties when I had them, and we were always broke. The library was a great place to hang out. Besides books and puzzles, they also had story time. And heat in the winter.

Phoenix was hot and dry and dusty year-round. As a kid, I walked the city. We didn't have a car, so we walked whenever the bus failed to show up. Even when the bus did show up, we'd often find ourselves walking long distances.

I walked our neighborhood, too, a perfectly flat rectangle that included the Christown shopping mall, where I occasionally ended up barefoot. Chlotene would turn me loose when I was bored. One day, she suggested I walk to the library, which hugged the south corner of the mall. It was the Yucca branch of the Phoenix Public Library.

Nobody had ever told me how the library worked. The building had a facade covered in massive stones, and as I walked in, I was hit with a wall of quiet, solemn as a church. Brown chairs and tables, brown shelves, brown carpet. I hesitated just on the other side of the front door. Even though at the time I didn't know what a country club was, I still felt like someone who sneaks into one and pretends to be a member. I took a few steps forward, and no one said anything. Since Chlotene had said it would be fine, I ventured in.

Because the children's books were kept in the back, I didn't even know the library had any. So I just paged through books that were left out on the big wooden tables in an open space near the stacks. After a half hour or so, I abandoned the books and left.

But I came back, over and over.

One day, as I was ferrying a book to the table, a librarian came up to me and asked, "Would you like to take that book home?"

I nodded, not sure if I had given the right answer. Was I in trouble?

"You'll need a library card. Do you have one?"

"No," I said, still not letting on that she was providing me with brand new information. "I don't have any money," I said, suspicious.

"Oh, no, they're free. They're free if you want one."

"OK. I want one," I said.

"Well, let's get you one," she said.

She walked me to the circulation desk and made a library card for me. Then she showed me where the children's section was so I could find more books I might be interested in reading. She showed me *Harold the Purple Crayon*. And she revealed to me that I could check the books out and take them home. I just had to remember to bring them back.

"Really?" I asked. "I can take these books home?"

"Yes, of course," she smiled.

I lugged my books home and told Chlotene, "Hey, Mom! I got these at the library. But I can't keep them; I have to take them back."

Over the following weeks, the same librarian took the time to show me the card catalog, and she often walked me back to the children's books section to help me find new books.

"I think you should read this book," she said, thumbing out *Pippi Longstocking* by Astrid Lindgren. "You're going to like it."

The *Pippi Longstocking* series became my favorite.

A girl with red hair, like me. Incredibly strong! She looked after herself, lived alone in a big broken-down villa and never went to school. She always had enough money (pure gold pieces that she hid in a closet in her house), and food was never an issue.

Her father was lost at sea, but she would see him again one day. Mom . . . dead.

Pippi gave me hope. The life of Pippi Longstocking seemed much more achievable to me than the family lives I saw advertised on TV. I didn't have superhuman strength like Pippi, but I had smarts like her. She outwitted cops and thieves, grownups, and other kids. Just like I often had to. It just seemed like her ability to outwit them always had a happier ending.

As a seven-year-old, Pippi was an inspiration for me. But when I look back, I see Chlotene resembled Pippi Longstocking much more than I did. Like Pippi, her life operated according to its own self-contained logic—a logic that was always shifting but also always made perfect sense to no one else but her.

> *Pippi was in the garden, watering the few flowers still in bloom with an old rusty watering can. As it was raining cats and dogs that day, Tommy told Pippi her watering seemed hardly necessary.*
>
> *"Yes, that's what you say," said Pippi grudgingly, "but I've lain awake all night thinking what fun it was going to be to get up and water, and I'm not going to let a little rain stand in my way."*[1]

In these first few years of my life, I felt confused a lot, but I didn't feel abnormal because Chlotene was my gauge for what was normal. I lived on the inside of our life, on the inside of our problems. Outside perspective hadn't arrived yet.

Even when I had inklings that something was weird, or I was just curious, I didn't know the "why" to most of it, even after I asked and Chlotene answered me.

Like when we moved. Sometimes we moved because we couldn't pay rent. Sometimes we moved because of Chlotene's paranoid delusions. Sometimes we just moved because we moved.

Asking Chlotene why we were moving was very much like asking Pippi Longstocking why she was watering her plants in the rain.

"I've lain awake all night thinking what fun it was going to be . . . and I'm not going to let a little rain stand in my way."

Chlotene minimized some delusions. Others she never voiced, or maybe she didn't think she had to. I didn't experience her delusions as hallucinations because I wasn't inside her head. Instead, her delusions were more like a worldview.

Just as I believe "normal" people can see the things that I see and hear the things I hear, Chlotene believed that the things she saw and heard were a shared reality that everyone else must be experiencing too.

When we lived in Phoenix, I didn't have anyone to compare notes with. She told me I was allergic to milk. So I never drank it. She also believed she was allergic to vegetables, so we never ate any. We had some canned green peas around, which she would boil to mush.

In the '70s in Phoenix, Chlotene got jobs as a waitress mostly. In those days, she went by Cleo, not Chlo or Chlotene.

In Phoenix it was Cleo. Then, in Columbus, her name somehow switched to "Chloe." Which eventually shortened to Chlo.

Chlotene's original birth certificate listed no first name. It was left blank. Chlo's parents' names were listed, as was Journey—their last name—and her date of birth. But they hadn't named her, or for some reason, hadn't bothered to fill out the birth certificate when she was born in 1940.

When she finally sent in the application to have her birth certificate corrected in the early 1980s, she showed it to me. It matched up with the story she had always told me.

"Oh, yeah," Chlotene would say. "My parents just called me 'honey bun.' My kindergarten teacher told me that I had to have a name and to go to the back of the room until I decided what my name was."

"So you picked Chlotene?" I asked.

"Yeah, I looked through the science books in the back of the room, and I liked the words. So I came up with the name Chlotene. Like chlorophyll."

That was her story. No name but the name she gave to herself.

Back in Phoenix, "Cleo" worked places that you might

compare to Mel's Diner from the TV show *Alice*, but without the TV sheen and the wisecracking "kiss-my-grits" Flo, and without the common sense or good judgment of Alice herself. If Chlotene was like anyone on that show, she was like Vera, trying to refill the straw dispenser at the counter but instead ripping open a box of straws so that they flew above her head like confetti.

In fact, she did have one very "Vera" moment that she told me about once. She was working during a dinnertime rush, with chaos in the kitchen.

"Drain the spaghetti!" one of the cooks barked at her. She'd never used a colander before. So she threw the spaghetti into the sink.

Schizophrenia made her scattered. Disorganized thinking "has been argued by some . . . to be the single most important feature of schizophrenia,"[2] according to the *Diagnostic and Statistical Manual of Mental Disorders, Fourth Edition*, where I read about it for the first time decades later when I was in graduate school.

Her disorganized thinking often put us in precarious straits. Once in a while, we'd get stranded far from any bus stop and have to flag down a stranger and ask for a ride. And we moved in with strangers when we had nowhere else to go.

She was rarely fired, but often she'd quit with no plan. Throughout her working life, and well into my adulthood, she never found another job before quitting the one she had, because the quitting didn't have much to do with whether or not she liked the job. In fact, she usually quit as soon as she found a place where the staff accepted her strangeness and found a way to work with it or around it. Her illness sabotaged her then, causing paranoia that got more and more intense until she would explode at a fellow waitress, a customer, or her boss. Then she would walk off the job, leaving bewildered co-workers in her wake who never saw it coming.

It's probably best to think of Chlotene as Pippi Longstocking but all grown up, with very long black hair hanging loose down her back and an untreated psychiatric illness. Then you have a closer approximation of my mother than any "normal" mom I can think of.

———

When I was that age in Phoenix—six, seven, eight years old—I thought the reason the way things were the way they were was because I didn't have a dad.

The reason we were always broke . . .

The reason I was home alone while my mom was out working . . .

The reason we didn't have enough food . . .

The reason life felt stressful and confusing and, most of all, unfair. All because I didn't have a dad. Most of all, life felt unfair. I knew I was being cheated.

When I was growing up, lots of kids lived with only their mom, like I did. But few of them had no contact with their dads whatsoever. For most of them, Dad was someone they saw a couple of times a year or every other weekend. Crucially, he was someone who gave Mom money.

That wasn't the case for me. I don't know who my biological father is. The story Chlotene told me was that he was her boyfriend, he set her up in an apartment, and when she got pregnant, he disappeared. She also told me that she ran into him in the grocery store once when I was a baby. I was in the cart, and she told him I was his, and he told her that that was impossible.

She told me that story once, when I was little. After that

conversation, my dad ceased to exist. His nonexistence was a fact—the way things had always been. I accepted it without question, the same way we hitchhiked and accepted strangers when the bus never came.

If I thought about him at all, I lumped in not knowing who he was with other oddities about my mother, like how somehow people were always getting into her mail and reading it, even though it was sealed when she got it from the mailbox. Or how Loretta Lynn was my mother's first cousin and not just a famous person we just happened to be watching on TV.

Since all of her weirdness sat tangled together in my mind, the solution got tangled up too. If life was like this because I didn't have a dad, then the solution must be that I needed to get a dad.

So I didn't think my biological dad would come back. But I wished for a dad all the time as a little girl. I wished for a dad so I could be more like other kids. I wished for a dad so that we could have enough money and enough food to eat. I wished for a dad so I could be safe from moving all the time, and from hiding under the sink, and from staying home alone. I'm not sure how to describe the level of longing and eventual grief I experienced as time went by. By the time I was twelve, I decided that I never needed a dad. I came to that conclusion as a matter of emotional survival.

But well before then, when we were still living in Phoenix, I still hoped for a dad.

One morning I woke up in our apartment, and a man was sleeping on the couch in the living room. I wasn't particularly surprised. It wasn't the first time that I woke up to find someone I had never met living with us.

I never witnessed Chlotene actually inviting someone to live with us, so I can't describe what those conversations were like. But it always felt sudden to me. Every time it happened, I discovered it the same way: I'd go to bed living with Chlotene and wake up living with Chlotene and someone else.

Likely, Chlotene met these strays at the diners where she worked. Even if I had witnessed the conversations, I doubt they would make these invitations or their acceptance seem more reasonable. Those people who were agreeing to live with her must not have had many—or any—other options.

A year or so before I woke up to the man on our couch, I woke up to Joan living with us.

When Joan moved in, we lived in a one-bedroom apartment facing the pool in a complex in Phoenix. We had lived there a few months, and I knew the complex well. I had already gone down all the alleys and climbed into all the tiny backyards by the time Joan arrived. I had even scrambled up onto the roof of our building. I'd collected aluminum cans and half-smoked cigarettes in the parking lot. I'd played in the back seats of people's cars.

One morning I woke up, and Joan was there. Chlotene and Joan seemed to have come to an arrangement that Joan could live with us in exchange for babysitting me. Or at least keeping an eye on me. Joan didn't play with me, and she didn't always feed me, but she was there in case I broke a leg or went missing for too long.

Joan smoked cigarette after cigarette in our apartment, so the ashtrays were always full to the brim. She regularly wore a mid-'70s muumuu, the shapeless house attire of the day.

Joan left a few months later, after Chlotene threw an explosive, hostile screaming fit.

It was a pattern I saw throughout my life. People would get comfortable with her "eccentricities," but that wasn't enough for her illness. In fact, their getting used to her seemed to stoke her paranoia.

I learned to fear her anger by watching her unleash it on others. I learned somehow to get out of the path—first physically, and then in some other way—so I could avoid the tsunami of her anger. I got better and better at anticipating it over the years because, like a tsunami, when you spot the wave, it's already too late to get out of the way.

I knew how to find indicators that she was likely to go off well before anyone else could tell. Even after years of practice, I didn't always spot it in time. Once when I was about twelve, I was playing with friends in their yard, but she couldn't find me. When she did finally find me, she discovered that I was having fun horseplaying and rolling around with the other kids on a blanket in the backyard. She dragged me away and beat the shit out of me on a busy street.

That was how her anger always felt, as out of the blue as the person who had come to live with us. Eventually, Chlotene's paranoid delusions would manifest as a blind rage that submerged and decimated everything in its path. Once people started to trust her, that was when her anger wrecked it all.

She would lose control mid-conversation. Knock the wind out of the other person with a flood of anger when they were relatively relaxed. If there was any warning at all, it was only visible to me as someone who spent a lot of time with her. She might purse her lips. Or let out a loud sigh. Or start to fidget. But before the target—or anyone else—had time to register those subtle signs, she was in their face, screaming and waving her hands around.

Joan, like many others, never saw it coming.

"YOU HAVE 24 HOURS TO PACK YOUR THINGS AND

GET OUT OF HERE!" Her voice was loud and low-pitched, like it was coming from a place deep inside.

"What? Why?"

"YOU KNOW WHY! STAY OUT OF MY MAIL! DON'T LET ME FIND YOU HERE TOMORROW, OR I'M CALLING THE COPS!" Chlotene screamed, her bulbous nose bright red.

Joan argued that she hadn't touched Chlotene's mail, but the denial just confirmed Chlotene's suspicions.

"I can't believe this!" Joan said.

"IF YOU SPENT MORE TIME LOOKING FOR A JOB AND LESS TIME WITH YOUR FINGER UP YOUR NOSE, MAYBE YOU WOULDN'T HAVE TO GO THROUGH MY MAIL!" Chlotene continued, her logic clear as day to no one but her.

"Fine!" Joan said, exasperated and trembling.

Joan was gone the next morning.

So by the time I woke up to this man sleeping on our couch, I was not, as I said, particularly surprised to see him. He was thin and balding, wearing a plaid work shirt and gray slacks.

I walked into the middle of the living room, which had no other furniture other than the couch he was lying on.

"Who are you?" I asked.

"I'm Billy," he said, turning over so that he faced the ceiling, his fingers fumbling a cigarette and a matchbook out of his shirt pocket.

"Hi. I'm Emily."

"Yeah," he said. "I'm a friend of your mom's."

"How'd you meet my mom?"

"We just met," he said, his hand making a kind of floating-ribbon gesture toward the front door, the lit cigarette pinched between his fingers.

"Oh," I said. "Are you gonna stay?"

"I love your mom," he said. "I'm gonna marry her. If she'll let me."

I can't say I was totally shocked by this announcement either, although I was a little more surprised by it than by finding him on our couch. And I was curious.

"Does that mean you're going to be my dad?" I asked.

"Do you want a dad?"

Chlotene came out of the bathroom and into the kitchen. She looked into the living room and said, "He's not my boyfriend." Addressing Billy, she said, "Stop it."

When I asked her later, she said, "No. We are NOT getting married."

He hung around for a few weeks, always sleeping on the couch, never in my mom's room, which was where I slept. Like Joan, he smoked, but unlike Joan, he punctuated his sentences with wild hand gestures, waving his cigarette around precariously. He almost burned me several times until he finally did burn me once, when the three of us were walking from the parking lot to the grocery store. He got me right above the belly button.

Pssssssss.

Chlotene was furious, I was screaming, and he blamed me for getting too close.

Not long after that, my mom told me he wasn't going to come around anymore. As Chlotene had said, Billy wasn't going to marry her. That meant he wasn't going to be my dad.

I was disappointed. Forlorn, even.

He wasn't going to buy us a car like he said he would. Or move us into a house. Or even take me to the zoo, a place I had always wanted to go. I had heard the other kids at school talk about the zoo for years and was delighted when he promised we'd go. It was finally going to be my turn.

I felt stranded. Even though I had enough sense to know

that Billy might not be all he was cracked up to be, I hoped that he would do all of those things he had promised. I hoped that he would change my life, and now I knew he wouldn't.

As a goodbye, he took me bowling. Then we went to Taco Bell, and he told me to get whatever I wanted from the menu, which I did. Then he didn't come around anymore.

Thinking about it over forty years later, I can't imagine why he didn't just disappear. Why did he go through the routine of taking me bowling and then to Taco Bell? It added a sense of finality that didn't befit his few-week-old relationship with Chlotene.

More than that, it was just so *responsible* of him. Billy, a homeless weirdo who slept on a stranger's couch and then claimed he was going to marry her, didn't leave the stranger's daughter wondering about what had happened.

In that very narrow and bizarre and stunted way, Billy did more for me than any other father figure in my childhood. He faced me. He felt like he owed me the truth.

"No, I won't be visiting again."

We were always the poorest people I knew, year after year. No matter how poor our neighbors were, we were poorer. Chlotene never filed for unemployment benefits when she was eligible, and she refused to apply for public assistance because she was paranoid that if she ever got "in the system," they'd remove me from her home. That was her greatest fear. As I look back now, I have to admit her paranoia about "them taking you away" was not the result of a delusion. At least not totally.

Chlotene had been hospitalized in 1964, six years before I was born, for her mental illness. She'd been released from

Central Ohio Psychiatric Hospital in 1965 as part of "deinstitutionalization," a process set into motion by the Community Mental Health Act of 1963. She didn't want to go back to be committed, and she worried that if she got on the radar of public assistance, she'd have to go back, and I'd be separated from her.

So if she wasn't working (which was often), we had absolutely no money. That meant that I often found myself tagging along with friends after school and then saying, "Ask your mom if I can stay for dinner!" I would sometimes ask to sleep over too.

We never had any fresh fruits or fresh vegetables. We had boxed mac and cheese but no butter or milk to mix into it. We had bare cupboards and only enough food in the fridge to fill one shelf, if that.

Even now, her cupboards and fridge look like this, not because she doesn't have enough money to buy food. Just because.

Sometimes I offer to take her out "wherever she wants." She always chooses McDonald's, where she'll order a Filet-o-Fish (hold the cheese and tartar sauce).

A mix of her illness and her pride also combined to form a belief in her that we didn't actually need any help. She felt like there were other people who *"really"* needed help and that she wasn't one of "those people," even though we were occasionally homeless and regularly had nothing to eat.

It wasn't that she wasn't smart. She was highly intelligent but with incredibly poor judgment. Chlotene had a combination of shame about accepting help, mistrust of anyone who might be poking around into her life asking questions, and also the disorganization that came with her severe, untreated mental illness.

I would see flashes of that toxic combo every once in a while. Once, when I was eight or nine, I remember the two of us helping a friend and her mom unload a trunk full of food they'd gotten at a local pantry. The food was in cardboard boxes. Even at that age, it struck me that this single mom was wealthy compared to us. She had a car! Yet she could ask for and receive free food, but we couldn't. One of the neighborhood kids came up to us, saw all the food, and asked, "Where were you?"

I had been so excited by all the groceries so neatly lined up—a rare sight in my life—that even though the food wasn't ours, I blurted, "We went to the pantry and got free food." As the word "food" left my mouth, I felt a violent blow to my cheek and saw stars. Chlotene had wheeled around and smacked me in the face as hard as she could.

I was stunned. I didn't see it coming, and of course, I felt shame. I didn't understand.

"Wha—what did I do?" I shrieked, although as I said it, my brain clicked on the explanation. My words had announced that I wished we could accept charity. I had announced it to another kid. And I had embarrassed my mom.

Because we moved so often in Phoenix, I went to at least half a dozen schools in four years. In the middle of third grade, I started at yet another school. I was always small and short for my age, and I have an April birthday. So when my mom told the school office that I was in second grade because she'd lost track of exactly what grade I was in, they placed me in second grade.

Of course, I wasn't with my mom for that conversation. If

I had been, I would have spoken up and told the administrators that I was actually in third grade.

I had to trail my mom often, correcting mistakes like that. Like an elf with a little broom and dustpan, I would open our mail so that we didn't lose bills. Rearrange our furniture (when we had furniture) so that it fit in our apartment. I was used to taking care of things.

But I wasn't there that day, so I couldn't speak up. Instead, I showed up for school and went to the classroom where I was told to go.

My mom really didn't care about school. She didn't care if I stayed home. She didn't think about grades and never looked at my report cards. Once I turned sixteen, she nagged me about dropping out so I could get a full-time job and help pay rent.

So it wasn't a huge surprise that she didn't know what grade I was in.

I didn't realize the mistake right away. It was the middle of the school year, so it wasn't like anyone was announcing which grade we were in while we were sitting in class.

But, as we opened our textbooks, I recognized it. I knew I'd already gone through it. I didn't say anything until the teacher assigned us one of the homework exercises. Then I raised my hand.

"Miss Graham, I've already done this homework."

"What do you mean?" said the teacher, sounding frazzled. She didn't like me interrupting.

"At my other school, we finished this book already."

"What *other* school?"

"At the school I was going to before, we read this book," I repeated.

"Uh-huh," she said, and her voice sounded like an eye roll. "It just looks the same."

"But I've already done this. I know what happens at the end!" I said.

"OK," she said. "Well, how far did you get in this book at your other school?"

I flipped the pages for a while, aware of the other kids' eyes on me. I held up a page near the end and pointed. "Here."

"OK, let's keep going. Emily, I'll look into this later," she said.

I let it drop.

The next day, I arrived at my desk and sat down. Miss Graham walked over and said quietly, "Emily, we're going to move you to the classroom next door." Third grade. "You'll have to work really hard to catch up," she said. As if she still couldn't believe I had completed second grade.

"OK," I said, suppressing the eye roll in my own voice.

I stayed at that school for about three more months before we moved again.

I got the last word a couple of years later. It was my last day living in Phoenix, which was also the last day that I attended school in Phoenix.

The day we left Arizona for good, I was nine years old and a few weeks into fourth grade. "We're moving to Ohio today," I told my teacher. "I won't be back here. I'm gonna miss you."

It was true: I would miss her. I had no friends because I hadn't been at the school long enough to make any. I was homeless at the time. She and her classroom were the only stable features of my life at a time when I was sleeping on the floor with my mom in a stranger's living room.

"That can't be right," she said. "If you were leaving, don't you think I would know about it?"

"You would?" I asked. But I recognized what was

happening here. I had learned by then that adults don't believe children. Especially adults with power to make a difference.

"Your mother would *have to* let us know. You can't just leave school one day and never come back! Go out to recess with the other kids."

That night my mother and I stepped on a Greyhound bus. I wouldn't set foot in Arizona again for twenty-one years.

2

RUTH ANN CAME to visit us in Phoenix in February 1979, when I was eight years old. She looked remarkably like Chlotene. They were only three years apart. Ruthie was the older sister, and she had black hair like Chlotene that she wore in a set bouffant that was old-fashioned even for the time. She wore almost the exact same oversized glasses as Chlotene. The major differences in their faces were that Ruthie had a thinner nose and two big front teeth that I saw a lot because she smiled a lot more than Chlotene did. Chlotene's teeth looked more uniform, but that was because they were dentures.

When Ruthie visited, we were living in one of our last apartments in Phoenix. The complex was designed in a U shape around the pool, and we could look straight out onto it whenever we opened the front door. Aunt Ruthie slept on the couch and took me to the pool every day, where she soaked up the Arizona sun and watched me swim.

For those nine years before Ruthie came to visit, Chlotene was not only all I had but all I imagined I had in the world. I thought I only had one family member—her. My mom's parents were dead. That was it. As far as I knew, Chlotene was my only connection.

She was surely the only person on Earth who would have missed me if I'd disappeared. We never received government assistance, didn't have health insurance, didn't own any property or a car. My mother had me enrolled in school but regularly pulled me out of one school and enrolled me in another without notice whenever we would move, which happened once or three times a year. Every time Chlotene made too many mistakes or acted so erratically that acquaintances or neighbors might get concerned enough to call any kind of authorities, we'd move.

Chlotene was the only one who would have missed me because she was often the only person on Earth who knew I existed.

Except for Roy and Eloise.

———

For a while, Roy and Eloise babysat me. They were an older couple with grown children of their own and a cat that I was supposed to leave alone but wouldn't.

We met them when I was five. Chlotene was about to start a new waitressing job, and she had no one to watch me during her shifts. She had seen Eloise tending to a crop of blooming rose bushes in the front yard of a tidy house.

So when she needed child care and didn't know where to go, she brought me to the front door and knocked.

Eloise answered the door. She was shortish and boxy, and while I don't remember exactly what she was wearing, I have more than a hunch that it was polyester. Polyester pants, a floral polyester shirt with a wide collar. Maybe even permed hair.

Chlotene introduced herself and told her she needed a babysitter. "Will you take care of Emily?"

I don't remember if my mother had told me what we were doing there, but I remember saying, "I promise I'll be good!"

For some reason, Eloise decided to say yes. She took me in. We watched *Wizard of Oz* together on TV. She tended to the scratches on my face left by the cat. She was good to me, and her husband was too. I don't know if Chlotene ever paid her.

A few months later, Easter fell on April 18, just a few days after my sixth birthday. Eloise had bought a new little white dress for me, with matching white socks and shoes, and an Easter basket. She'd also gotten me a birthday cake. I'd never had any of those things before.

Years later, as I was approaching my thirtieth birthday, I asked myself, *Did that . . .? Did that really happen the way I remember it?*

My memory of Roy and Eloise was gauze-covered. It was almost too vivid—as though it could have been a dream. I had only been five years old. Did we literally walk up to the house and ring their doorbell one day? Could that be how Chlotene met them? Maybe they knew each other in some other way.

I had a deeper worry, too, a worry that I didn't want to voice to myself. What if I had made them up? Or if I hadn't made them up, what if I'd made up their kindness? A gentle older couple who had looked after me? Who had cared about me?

I had no reliable witnesses. Nowhere to go to confirm my memories.

I could have asked Chlotene, but her refrain when I asked

her about the past was "I don't remember" and "Why are you asking me about that?"

So much of my reality existed in my own head and nowhere else. Even if Chlotene had not been so inflexible about reminiscing or answering questions, how could I rely on what she remembered? On what she told me was happening? The things that were happening to her took place in a reality I could not experience.

I had my reality, living in my own head. But no other reliable connection to my past. What had actually happened?

Then, one day, I found my mom's old address book. I paged through it to see if I recognized any names from the past. The names were faded, but there they were—Roy and Eloise—with their full names scribbled in pencil. I decided to find them.

It was 1999, before the proliferation of Google, so I went to the main library in Columbus and got my hands on a Phoenix phone book. I mailed a letter to everyone with their last name. The letter included a photo of me in their front yard, standing in front of the rose bushes in the white Easter dress. In the letter I described what I remembered and ended by saying, "You were really important to me. I'd like to say thank you." And I included my phone number.

I started to get responses.

"Hey, this is so nice. It's not me, but I hope you find them!"

Then I got a call from their son. He had received a letter. He said, "Yeah, they remember you! I remember you! We loved having you, and then you and your mom just disappeared one day. We never knew what happened to you. We were worried."

He put his mother on the phone, and with the first words out of her mouth, I knew I had not imagined her.

"Hello, honey," Eloise said. "We got your letter. We were so worried about you! You just disappeared."

Chlotene hadn't said goodbye, which wasn't unusual for her. They had been worried, and they had always wondered. They *had* cared, they said.

Eloise said she wanted me to come see them. I knew I would.

The following month, I took a trip out to Phoenix with my husband Tim to revisit the library where I'd checked out *Pippi Longstocking*, the shopping mall where I hung out barefoot, and a couple of our old apartment buildings.

And I saw Roy and Eloise too.

We had large swaths of life to catch up on, of course. They were still married but lived in a different house in a different part of town. I had an entire youth's worth of news to share. I was married. I had children. I had a house of my own.

"What about Cleo?" Eloise asked, calling Chlotene by the name she'd used in Phoenix. At the time my mom was stable, living on her own and working in Columbus, and that's what I told them.

"She's fine," I said.

Eloise told me about meeting Chlotene for the first time. It was true Chlotene had marched up to their front door with me in tow and knocked. Eloise remembered that first encounter. She knew Chlotene had nothing. No money. No people. No support.

When we disappeared, they had looked for us, Eloise said. They had visited the apartment complex where they knew we lived. We had moved out, though, and no one they asked knew where we had gone.

But not being family, they couldn't get anywhere with the police. They didn't have enough evidence to file a missing person's report.

No one else in my life besides my mom could do something like file a missing person's report if I'd disappeared.

So when Ruth Ann, my mother's older sister, came to Phoenix, my whole world changed. Not only was Ruthie related to me—*family*—but she also had two daughters of her own. I had cousins.

And I found out that in Columbus, my mother had been married and had four other children.

I had siblings.

Every day that Ruthie stayed with us, I learned something new about my family. I asked her questions, and she'd give me answers. Real answers that made sense. She wasn't scary or guarded, and I felt genuine love from her immediately.

She was the one who told me my siblings were a lot older than me, so they probably wouldn't play with me much. She was the one who told me that not only did I have siblings, but Ruthie herself had a family with a husband and children. An uncle. Cousins.

After ten years of staying out of contact with her relatives in Ohio, who didn't know if she was alive or dead, Chlotene was running out of the energy she needed to live on her own, towing me around.

As the time for Ruthie to leave drew closer, I overheard the two of them talking quietly about whether I should go back with her. Chlotene decided not to send me, and I was devastated. I wanted to go.

Ruthie drove us in her rental car to the airport so we could see her off. I pressed my nose against the glass after she'd boarded her plane. I was crying inconsolably, spitting and squirting all over the window, my hands pressed against the glass. But I didn't argue with Chlotene. It was time to go, and we had to figure out how to get the bus back.

I didn't know it yet, but Ruthie had convinced my mother to return to Columbus "soon."

My mother, Chlotene Journey, was born with no name in Portsmouth, Ohio, on the other side of the Ohio River from West Virginia.

Her father died when she was sixteen and her mother when she was nineteen, not long after Chlotene had gotten married. Both of her parents died when they were forty. Rhoda, her mother, had cancer.

Chlotene's father was a truck driver and was often not home. Her mother worked as a seamstress, assembling shoes. She and her younger brother were alone at home a lot, even at ten or eleven. One evening, while walking home from work, Chlotene's mother was grabbed off the sidewalk and raped.

Chlotene has a memory of the police coming to the door. Just she and her seven-year-old brother Ronald were home.

"They were wondering where my family was," Chlotene said. Ruth Ann wasn't home. Her mother was in the hospital. She didn't return home for two weeks. When she came back, she had changed. "She was in bed a lot," Chlotene told me. "My mom needed my comforting," she added.

They moved from Portsmouth and bought a house in Whitehall, a suburb of Columbus. A few years passed. And then . . .

"I came home from a friend's house," Chlotene told me. "My mom was in the bathroom with my dad. He had fallen and hit his head. My mom shouted at me to call an ambulance."

Her father died that day of a cerebral hemorrhage.

"Well, I'm all talked out," she said when she told me these stories, fact by fact, in the fall of 2020 in a phone call. I had told her I wanted to know about my grandparents. "Your parents," I said, making sure to clarify what I meant. I had heard bits and pieces of these stories before, but I'd never sat and had a conversation with her about her childhood.

Talking about the past has always made her anxious. When I was a child, we never talked about life before Arizona. When I was an adult, we never talked about Arizona. If I tried to ask more than one question in a row, Chlotene made it clear to me that I wasn't reminiscing. I was prying.

Back then, clamming up was, of course, related to her paranoid delusions. Sometimes. Or maybe she felt shame, or maybe her brain was so disorganized that trying to recall specific memories from a time and a place overwhelmed her. Whatever it was, she was driven to escape.

But this day was a good day. I found she was able to hold a short conversation and answer my questions. She was sitting in her glider rocking chair. I could hear squeaking as she rocked. The squeak would pause as she would tense up. At one point, I could barely hear her, and I told her that I didn't catch all of what she'd just said.

Instead of repeating herself, she said something in an even quieter monotone. She didn't want to repeat what she'd said originally. Something about her mother yelling at her brother and her while they were playing.

But she didn't hang up or cut me off, so that was good. She knew that I wanted to hear, and she didn't retreat into "Let's forget the past" or "I don't remember."

The first time I ever had an extended conversation with Eric Tubbs was in 2020, when he was eighty-three years old. I'd known him for years but had barely ever exchanged more than a few words with him. When I met him in a Waffle House in September, he was hard of hearing, and he took care with his appearance, as he always had. He was tall, trim, and clean-cut. His hair was parted to the right and combed down, gray and thinner than it had been, but it was still lying dutifully across his scalp, just like in his wedding photo.

Chlotene had married Eric back in 1958. He'd met her at church in Whitehall. He said that Chlotene's mother had warned him that Chlotene was "mentally deficient" and very impulsive. I don't think her family would have known what schizophrenia was back then, even if they suspected that Chlotene had it. At the onset of Chlotene's schizophrenia in the late 1950s, mental illness was stigmatized. "Stigmatized" is an understatement. Mental illness wasn't even called "mental illness." It was called "being nuts." Maybe "mentally deficient" when talking to a nice young man like Eric at church.

Chlotene's mother made it to their wedding and died of cancer within two months.

By July 1960, Chlotene was twenty with two dead parents, a two-year-marriage, and two children of her own. The young family took a road trip to Pennsylvania to see his family. When Chlotene met his sister, Eric said she became uncontrollably jealous.

"She got real mad about the way my sister was hugging me," Eric said as more coffee was delivered to our table at the Waffle House.

So mad, and so jealous, that she picked up her suitcase

and hitchhiked back to Columbus, five hundred miles away. Without her children. Eric understood what Chlotene's mom had meant by "mentally deficient."

They had two more children before Chlotene filed for divorce in 1963.

She got the house, the four kids, the nicer of the two cars, and twenty-five dollars a week in child support. Not enough to pay all their bills and the mortgage. Eric told me he knew that Chlotene wouldn't be able to handle the responsibilities. He was proved right: a year later, she asked him to take the house back. They went back to court, and Eric was granted the house and the kids. Chlotene kept the car.

"I didn't know what she did after that," Eric said.

Chlotene had always told me she left the kids behind because she couldn't afford to take care of them, which was true. Even the most organized and conscientious twenty-three-year-old mother of four young children with no family support would have had trouble supporting them.

But she wasn't conscientious. She was in the throes of a severe mental illness. She was not receiving treatment even as the paranoid delusions that came along with her illness made it impossible for her to connect directly to the reality the rest of us agree on.

Eventually she got so confused, so driven by her own version of reality, that she had to leave.

It was the beginning of a pattern Chlotene repeated over and over.

She couldn't live in the same place for too long before her delusions inhabited the place too. The neighbors were breaking in when she wasn't around. They were opening mail. Old boyfriends were driving by. Perhaps she had other delusions that didn't come out of her mouth but forced her, like a constant, persistent shoving, to move along. She couldn't keep the same job for too long before her coworkers were plotting or whispering or in cahoots with her prying neighbors.

They all wanted something; they were following her. She had to go. Certainly without a plan for where to go next and always without warning.

Whenever we would move when I was growing up, she never even tried to sell whatever wasn't coming with us. She would leave it on the sidewalk or give it away, like she did with the three-piece living room furniture set. The state of having things would overwhelm her, and she would give the things up. Things, and I guess people too.

After Chlotene gave up custody, Eric didn't hear from her until nearly a year later, in 1964, when he got a call from an FBI agent in Indiana. Chlotene had been picked up hitchhiking on the side of the highway. She had a stolen ID on her—a flight attendant's ID. She was in jail. So Eric decided to go to Indiana and pick her up. At first she refused help, he said, but changed her mind after a couple of more weeks in jail.

So Eric asked the judge to grant a transfer to the Central Ohio Psychiatric Hospital in Columbus. The judge had her transferred to the hospital. She didn't follow up on treatment and disappeared from the lives of Eric and her kids.

The only way I found out Chlotene had ever been hospitalized was through a flip comment made decades later, probably around 1994. My half-sister Linda told me, "Dad would drive us by the hospital and say, 'That's where your mom lives!'" A flip comment about the memory of a flip comment.

Other than that, her four kids didn't see or hear of her for sixteen years, from 1963 until 1979. The younger ones didn't even remember her.

But in 1979, when I was eight years old and we were still living in Phoenix, I didn't know all that. All I knew was what

I was gleaning from overhearing Chlotene and Ruthie chatting: I had family in a place called Ohio. I had a brother and three sisters who all lived with their dad who was not my dad.

And I couldn't wait to meet them.

A few months after Ruthie left, we moved out of our apartment.

We were running again. Chlotene had lost her job and couldn't make rent that month. We weren't evicted. Eviction takes months. Time was up for Chlotene, and she needed to go now. Her brain just wouldn't let her stay.

At nine years old, I had to go, too, of course. So we packed our things in a borrowed suitcase and boxes from the grocery store, left the keys on the kitchen counter, and just like that, we were homeless. We spent our last couple weeks in Phoenix in the living room of a man's one-bedroom apartment.

I guess you could've called it "couch surfing" if Chlotene hadn't had a nine-year-old in tow. She slept on the couch. I slept on the bare floor next to the couch. As soon as we landed there, Chlotene called her sister Ruth Ann and told her she wanted to come home now. Ruth Ann wired money and bus tickets so that we could get to Columbus.

Why did this stranger allow us to "crash" with him? Maybe he was doing Chlotene a favor. Maybe her complete lack of boundaries attracted other people who also had a complete lack of boundaries. We had to sleep somewhere.

She talked about her decision to move out with a sense of pride mixed with a blithe disregard for the idea that she might stay in a place until she was actually evicted. "Eviction," like "eligible" and "qualified for assistance," wasn't part of her vocabulary.

But her pride was an afterthought, anyway. Her pride wasn't what dragged around Phoenix all those years.

The truth was that her paranoia worsened each day she stayed in the same place. She only needed the flimsiest of excuses to erase everything and start all over. Whenever she moved or quit a job without having another one lined up, it was like she was shaking an Etch A Sketch.

Whenever life became messy and overwhelming, she would just shake the circumstances of her life away to start again. Unable to draw the picture she wanted, she would start over in another place. At another job. With another friend. At another church. And later, I found out, with another pregnancy.

The moves felt normal to me as a kid because Chlotene never seemed panicked when she delivered her decision. She felt sure that going was the answer, and she always framed our next move like it was going to be the one that would keep us safe. We were lucky! We could finally get away from our crazy neighbor and start fresh.

On top of that, whenever we moved, her paranoia *did* abate for a while, which meant I felt relief too. She was OK for a while, which meant I could be OK too. Every move also meant I would be switching schools, which I welcomed when I was younger because I was often bullied for being small and poor and unkempt. I could even think of each move as an adventure. As I approached high school, though, I got sick of moving. I was happy with my school, and I didn't want to lose my friends. I finally put my foot down.

"You can move, but I'm not going with you," I told Chlotene when she wanted to move out of my high school's district when I was sixteen. She was angry about it. She was sure we were risking our safety. But she knew I meant it, so we stayed put until I graduated.

Years later, after I'd married my first husband, Tim, but before I had kids of my own, Chlotene bought a house in Columbus. She had a relatively stable period during this time; she held down a job at AT&T and had a car, so she didn't have to rely on the bus to get her there.

It all fell apart when she quit the job because "They're trying to find reasons to fire me." At the same time, she didn't want to be saddled with the mortgage, so she stopped making payments.

She found an apartment and moved into it. Then she called the bank and left the house keys on the kitchen counter. She was already moving when she called to tell me the news.

I was twenty years old at the time. I told her, "Mom, even if you don't pay the mortgage, it'll take them a year to foreclose! Why don't you just stay and save up some money?"

I was remembering our life in Phoenix. How we moved out of apartments and became homeless, even though we weren't being evicted. We left the keys on the counter and walked away, even though we could have had a place to live if we had just stayed.

But we didn't. When we lived in Phoenix and moved suddenly, I just accepted it. But now that I was out of her house and watching her do this to herself, I found myself irate. Her decision—all her decisions—enraged me. Why was she doing something that caused so much upheaval so unnecessarily? I wanted to shake the crazy out of her.

Why are you making your life more difficult? I wanted to

shout at her as a twenty-year-old just embarking on a life of my own. *Why are you doing this?*

But, as always, I'd found out after the deal was made. The lease was already broken or a new lease was already signed. Job was already quit. Money was already squandered on a scam. Keys were already left on the counter.

———

That's how it was during our last days in Phoenix, September 1979.

It was the beginning of fourth grade. We moved into the living room of that man she'd met . . . somewhere. Probably at work. She needed a place to crash, and he said OK. Chlotene slept on the couch, while I slept on the tile floor between the coffee table and the couch. Every couple of days, he would ask about our prospects for finding a place of our own.

He lived in a forgettable apartment. The front door opened onto the living room, the couch on the right, kitchen on the left. Then a bathroom and one bedroom.

I didn't hang out there much or eat there. I was in school, and when I wasn't, I was asking friends if I could hang out at their houses. Hang out and maybe stay for dinner too. I know now his apartment must have been filthy. If it smelled bad, I didn't notice. I probably smelled bad.

The man had a girlfriend who usually stayed over. She was a blond with shoulder-length curly hair. One night he was in bed watching TV with two women, one on either side of him.

They were giggling. Before he closed the door, Chlotene leaned her head down from the couch and whispered to me,

"That is not normal. There are not supposed to be two women. It's just *one* man and *one* woman."

Of course, the whole thing was "not normal." Except that it was.

I reach my arm down into deep, black waters and pull out memories covered in clinging layers of algae.

One layer is the algae of what I told myself was happening at the time. Another layer is all the other memories of not-normal moments that were such a normal part of my childhood. They were mundane. Memories of us hitchhiking and accepting rides from strangers.

Other memories of us homeless and sleeping in someone else's living room—Chlotene on the couch, me on the floor. September 1979 wasn't the first time, and it wouldn't be the last time either.

Another layer: My feelings now about that moment sleeping on this strange man's floor back then. I know now, forty years later, that I was in a chaotic situation. I know it intellectually. But I don't feel it because reality wasn't chaotic for Chlotene. She lived in a skewed reality that seemed upright to her. When I was a child, I inhabited that skewed reality too.

Even as an adult, I often slid back into her reality without warning. Like the time when I was twenty-six, and I found out that Chlotene had once given birth to a boy, Edward. She was in prison in West Virginia in 1966, three years before I was born.

I found out about him because his foster mom called her in 1996, and Chlotene called me the same day. She told me everything: he existed, she'd had him after her four kids with her ex-husband but before me, and she'd had him in prison. That, at the time, she had been serving a sentence for grand theft auto.

"You're going to be mad at me," she said when I answered the phone.

That was how she always opened conversations where she was breaking news. Not "I did something" or "I have to tell you something," but a warning about my reaction.

Was she in the hospital? Did she hurt someone? I wanted her to get to the point quickly so I could know how upset I needed to be.

"You know about the kids I had with my ex-husband Eric."

"Yes."

"Well, before I had you, I had another baby." She started crying. "His mother called me. She said she's been helping him look for me for a long time." Her voice took on a pleading tone. "I don't want to meet him, Emily."

"OK. Wait a second. I need you to go back and tell me what happened."

She did. She told me she'd stolen a car to get away from her abusive boyfriend and had gotten caught. That's how she'd ended up in prison.

I met her son Edward a few times but never got to know him very well.

Another twenty-five years passed. I brought up prison and Ed in 2021, when I was trying to remember the details for this book.

"I don't remember any of that," she told me over the phone. "I remember meeting Edward at your kitchen table."

"Remind me, how long were you in prison again back in 1966?" I asked her.

"Well, that was just a charity thing. I was just in prison

while I was pregnant, and then after I had the baby, they let me out."

"Oh," I said, not reacting to the fact that that couldn't be true, and that anyway, it wasn't the story she had told me when Ed surfaced twenty-five years ago. She told me she'd had him in prison. That she'd had scarlet fever, which caused him to be born deaf. That she was afraid of her boyfriend, the baby's father, and glad that at least in jail, he couldn't get to her.

"They put me in jail as charity because my boyfriend was abusing me, and I didn't have any place to live."

"Oh," I said. "So what did they charge you with?"

"They never charged me with anything."

"Mom," I said, "they had to charge you with something in order to put you in prison."

"No," she insisted. "It was different back then."

Fifty-five years since delivering Ed in prison. Twenty-five years since meeting him as an adult for the first time. Six years since starting a regular medication regimen.

It's not forgetfulness. I know it's not forgetfulness because of the stories she'd shared with me just a few months before about her own childhood. It's not forgetfulness; it's her reality.

I reacted to her reality the way I always have. I know there's no clawing her out. There's no reaching down into the depths and dragging her out. She's afraid of something, and that fear keeps her down there. What is she afraid of? I don't know.

All I know is that if I ask for more, plunge ahead, challenge her story, ask if we can go over the details again, she'll clamp her jaw shut and dive down as deep as she has to until I let her go. And I don't want to go there with her, so . . . I let go.

I changed the subject, and we chatted about my daughters.

After I hung up the phone, I went over the conversation in my mind. Even though my intention in calling Chlotene that day was to try to get a better sense of what prison was like for her, my changing the subject when she wouldn't answer my questions was a reflex. I hardly realized I was doing it until I hung up the phone.

What was that? I thought, kicking myself. I reached for the phone. I wanted to call her back.

But I didn't. Because if I had called back, I would have asked again what prison was like and whether it made her afraid. But she doesn't live in a reality where she can talk clearly about ever having been in prison.

Chlotene had stuffed it all in her purse. The money and the bus tickets that Aunt Ruthie had sent us so we could get to Columbus.

At some point, a couple of days before our scheduled bus trip, the money disappeared. Chlotene left the room to go to the bathroom and left the money in her purse. When she came back, it was gone.

I came home from school that day. The TV was on, flickering in the dark bedroom. The blond was sitting in the kitchen just to my left as I walked in.

Before I could ask where Chlotene was, the blond said, "Your mom's in the bathroom. You should go in there."

So I did.

In the bathroom, Chlotene was crying and distraught, sitting on the edge of the bathtub.

I often needed to comfort Chlotene. I knew what to do. I sat next to her and put an arm around her.

"What happened?" I asked.

"They stole my money," she sobbed. "I don't have any money now."

I gasped. "We're not gonna be able to go to Ohio?" I asked.

"Oh, well, no, Emily. They left the tickets," she said. "They just took the money."

"Who?" I asked.

"One of them," she said as she motioned with her hand to the kitchen on the other side of the wall.

She could hardly speak through her tears. I had never seen her so distraught. I had seen her angry, but not torn up into a thousand pieces of defeat like this. Her face was red and splotchy from her hard crying. She blew her round nose and wiped her tears with her hand.

I handed Chlotene her glasses, which she'd perched on the sink. "Everything's going to be fine, Mom. We don't need money! We can still get to Columbus."

She put the glasses on and sniffled. "But the money's gone. All of that money Ruthie gave me is gone!"

"How? What happened to the money?" I asked.

"I left it in my purse, and one of them went into my purse and stole it," she said quietly, afraid the blond in the kitchen would hear.

"Mom. It's gonna be OK."

"What are we gonna do for food?" she asked.

It was a good question.

"Maybe they'll let us take some food," I said. "Or maybe they'll let us borrow some money." As a nine-year-old, it didn't register how absurd it would be for them to lend us money they'd just stolen from us.

But they did lend her money. They gave her ten dollars, and Chlotene ended up using that to buy bread and peanut butter. She made a stack of sandwiches for us, and we went to sleep.

Chlotene slept on the couch with her purse that night, even though there wasn't any money left in it. Just the bus tickets.

It took me a long time to fall asleep, like a kid on Christmas Eve. My mood completely contrasted against Chlotene's anxiety and distraught defeat. We were moving to a place where I had a family! I was going to meet *four* siblings. And I was going to see Aunt Ruthie again.

The next morning, I got up, went to school, and then found my way to the bus station. We spent three days and nights on the bus from Phoenix to Columbus.

"We're going to see the Grand Canyon," Chlotene promised. She kept saying it, hours after we had already crossed into New Mexico.

A woman named Louise gave us a little money, so we ate more than peanut butter sandwiches for at least a couple of meals. In between stops, I ran up and down the bus aisle like the bratty little nine-year-old I was.

Once I was using the bathroom and saw Chlotene's false teeth soaking in a cup on the sink. I shouted to her from the bathroom, "Mom! You left your teeth in here!" The whole bus ignited in laughter. Although she didn't have enough shame *not* to leave her teeth in the bus bathroom, the laughter did make her turn bright red and grit her toothless jaw at me.

I couldn't wait to meet my three sisters and brother. Instead, we met Aunt Ruthie and two gawky teenage girls, one with short brown hair and the other with long wavy blond hair. We piled into Ruthie's conversion van. I sat in the chair behind the front seat, and the girls sat behind me, in the third row, side by side. As we pulled out of the parking lot, I turned to face them.

"Are you my sisters?" I asked. They giggled but didn't say anything.

Ruthie said, "Oh, no, honey! These are your cousins, Diane and Judy. Girls, say hi to your cousin Emily," Ruthie sang out cheerfully.

I didn't meet my half-siblings for weeks after that. I spent the first month or so getting settled in Columbus, staying with Aunt Ruthie and daydreaming about what it would be like when I finally got to meet them. I'd always envied friends who had siblings. I'd even envied the petty arguments: "That's mine! Give it back!" I guess I envied their familiarity. They could bicker and fight, and when it was all over, they still had each other.

Their apartments seemed full of sound and scent and aliveness that we didn't have in ours. They had pictures on their walls. Toys. The mess of a nest that nurtured its hatchlings. I longed for that kind of home life, and I thought that family members would make me a nest.

When I met my siblings several weeks later, it was awkward, of course. All the more awkward because the meeting was such a mismatch with my fantasy.

We met at Ruthie's house, where they filed in and hugged Chlotene robotically. They didn't seem to take much interest in me at all. They didn't even make eye contact with me.

In my fantasy, we would talk for hours. Just me and my cool older siblings! The eldest, Theresa, was twenty, and the youngest, John, was almost seventeen. They would ask all sorts of questions about where we'd been and what Phoenix was like, and I'd ask about Ohio. Beyond that, I'm not sure what else my nine-year-old brain expected. Laughter and love and some kind of resolution, like the thirty-minute TV sitcoms that dominated the airwaves at the time, I guess.

For them, it all must have been very painful. After more than a decade, they were seeing a stranger. A mother who had been out of their lives, who had been in jail and institutionalized, and who had finally abandoned them. Now she was showing up out of the blue after years of no contact.

In the interim they'd grown up. In the interim she'd birthed and was raising another child.

Why had my mom kept me but left her four other children behind?

"I needed to keep one," was all she told me later. Years later I found out that I had two more half-siblings whom she'd given up for adoption before she got pregnant with me. Seven children for her. Six half-siblings in all.

3

As I was growing up, it wasn't like one day I realized my mom actually suffered from paranoid schizophrenia. It dawned on me gradually.

Oh, my mom isn't normal. My mom is weird.

But then again, everyone thinks their mom is weird, especially at the beginning of adolescence, which is when I started to think it quite seriously.

Her weirdness was obvious. Her illness was easy to minimize and dismiss. In Ohio, the other adults around never said Chlotene might be sick. They called her nuts on occasion, but they threw the word around like it meant "eccentric." The topic didn't belong in polite, everyday conversations. It was to be avoided whenever possible. Tolerated only when it couldn't be avoided. Since no one openly acknowledged Chlotene's mental illness, no one ever mentioned that our situation—her raising me alone—might not be safe.

In 1965 Chlotene left the psychiatric hospital where her ex-husband Eric had had her committed. It seems dramatic to say, but the Community Mental Health Act that President

Kennedy had signed into law in 1963 played a huge role in what happened in Chlotene's life once she left the hospital. That law began the largest exit of severely mentally ill people from institutions . . . without any community support. While the intention of the law was to address the lack of community support, the development of a support infrastructure was years down the road. In the meantime, mentally ill people were reinstitutionalized in prisons and ghettos. Chlotene was free to leave the hospital, but she didn't receive the follow-up support that she needed. Instead, my mom was among the women who turned to prostitution and abusive men to survive.

She got pregnant twice after she left the psychiatric hospital and before she got pregnant with me. The first time was in 1966, with Edward. She had birthed him in prison in August and surrendered him immediately. Ed grew up in foster families and was never adopted. The second time was in February of 1969. Michelle, my sister, whom I met in 1998 after she hired a private detective to find her birth mother and then found all of us too. It was two weeks after she surrendered Michelle for adoption that Chlotene spent the last of her money to move to Phoenix.

In 1970, fourteen months after Michelle was born, I became my mom's last and seventh child.

I was born into a reality that I saw as fixed. Then it began to shift, and I couldn't be sure what was real.

I thought I was an only child. (Yes. But then, years later, *no*.)

Neighbors were trying to get into our apartment and open our mail. (Yes and no.)

It was just me and my mom. (Yes.)

It was just me and my mom. (*No. It was just me and my mom and her secrets and her illness.*)

As a child in Phoenix, I didn't know anything different. People throw around that phrase: "I didn't know anything different."

But Chlotene lives on one side of a gauzy sheet that separates her reality from actual reality. Before I hit adolescence, I lived on that side of the sheet too. But I started to see everyone else through the haze of that gauzy sheet. She couldn't explain to me why she couldn't see them.

For example, the allergies.

She told me she was allergic to things. Like air. Not pollen. She believed she was allergic to the air itself, and so she couldn't go outside. She often didn't go outside for days at a time.

I was allergic to milk, she told me. I accepted that, no problem. Until I didn't accept it anymore. I'd be over at a friend's house, drink some milk, and not get sick. Not only that, but everything about their houses caused me to pierce the gauze. I saw their fridges and cupboards, so different from mine at home. My friends were poor, like us, but somehow, they had milk and maybe even orange juice in the fridge. Butter. Ice cream in the freezer. Bananas on the counter. I saw so much abundance.

I drank the milk, and I didn't get sick. Other families had something that we didn't. They were poor, too, but they had food, and most of it even tasted good. Why didn't we have that?

Something was wrong with my mom. She was more than just an impulsive person with a big mouth. She was more than a hothead.

The summer between sixth and seventh grade, when we'd been living in Columbus for two years, two guys in suits came to our apartment and invited us to their church. I had shown up at an evening Bible class a few weeks earlier and had filled out an information card with our address. They must have read "Save me" between the lines when they fished it out of the children's offering plate. We started to go to that church, a two-story brick building called Barnett Road Baptist Church.

I met Kylee there. She was a grade ahead of me, and she pulled me into the youth group. At twelve years old, it was one of the first stable groups of friends I'd ever had. Kylee saved me in ways that church itself really couldn't. I lived alone with my mom and didn't see my other family members much at all. We had a little black-and-white TV at that time that got three channels. We didn't have a phone. No Google. Kylee was a friend to connect me to the outside world.

Church provided me with friends. Youth group often took place in other people's homes, where I got exposed to versions of family life that I suspected but hadn't had a lot of chances to see for myself. I walked into homes with comfy living room furniture. Even if it didn't all match, it all belonged in the living room. My friends had sheets on their beds.

One of the church members, Jeanine, was a frequent volunteer who had let me come to work with her for a couple of weeks one summer at the Southern Baptist Convention. She told me that she would pay me, and she did. Twenty dollars for a solid two weeks of filing and cleaning and sticking stickers to religious literature. A measly twenty bucks! At the time, I remember, I was livid. As a twelve-year-old, I was smart enough to know I'd been cheated. Now I realize she was probably doing Chlotene a favor, keeping me busy for a while.

One Sunday later that year, we were just inside the entrance to our church. Jeanine was bending down to organize a stack of leaflets that she was going to leave on display.

Chlotene started to scream.

"Stop sticking your ASS up in the AIR. I KNOW WHAT YOU'RE DOING. YOU'RE TRYING TO SLEEP WITH THE PASTOR!"

Which sounds pretty crazy, and it was. It wasn't just the words she used. She saw red. She got so loud, out of nowhere. She was cute until she wasn't, like a teddy bear with fangs.

People could dismiss or tolerate her delusions as eccentric until the delusions twisted into some strange sexual perversion or violent imagining. Until they weren't about the person in front of her. She morphed from strange to stunning. Stunning as in the way a taser is stunning.

After that run-in, another adult at church pulled me aside and whispered in my ear, "There's something wrong with your mom."

Duh! I thought but didn't say. *Of course there's something wrong with her!*

I was going to find an escape from my life, no matter what. I was getting *out*. I guess, looking back, I'm grateful my escape was church and not drugs or petty theft. Church provided the answer to everything as long as I accepted that the answer to everything was Jesus. So I did accept it.

I decided I wanted to be baptized. I'd seen other people

do it, and I was ready for the full dunk. The Barnett Road church did a full-body dunk on Sunday during the service. The baptismal font was a glass-walled tub up on a stage behind the pulpit, with hidden steps that led down into the font. The person getting baptized would walk down these steps just "off-stage," and from the congregation you'd see them appear in the water, as if by magic.

Back at home the night before my baptism, I looked at the white polyester choir robe the church had given me to be baptized in. We lived in the only two-story apartment we'd ever lived in, and I called up the stairs.

"Mom, am I supposed to wear clothes under this thing?"

She yelled at me from the top of the stairs. "Of course you wear clothes!"

And then—

"WHAT'S WRONG WITH YOU?? ARE YOU TRYING TO GET RAPED? ARE YOU TRYING TO HAVE SEX?"

I looked up and yelled back, "What. Are. You. Talking. About?"

"WHY DO YOU WANT TO BE NAKED UNDER THERE?"

"Of course I don't wanna be!"

My face flushed red. The conversation ended there.

I shut down and ran out of the apartment. She had laid something on me that I had to get off, like slime. I couldn't even believe her mind would go there, even though I didn't even fully understand where her mind was going. It was appalling. It was the furthest thing from what I was thinking or what I was asking about.

Once I hit puberty, we had exchanges like that regularly. It was absolutely common for her to accuse me of wanting to have sex or be raped. These were the kinds of moments that started to accumulate against a dam in my mind, like runoff from a rainstorm.

She isn't right, I started to think.

We were poor, and we didn't have things, and I didn't have a dad, and yes, those things were true of so many of our neighbors and my friends at school. But. Something else was going on.

I didn't just feel angry. I felt ashamed. Ashamed of her. Ashamed that she was my mom.

When my sister Carol, Chlotene's second child, moved in with us in the summer of 1983, we lived in that same two-bedroom, two-story apartment in a huge complex in Whitehall.

The complex was crawling with kids my age, so I had friends to hang out with that summer after seventh grade. Our apartment had a front door *and* a back door. It even had a screen door. It was quite a decent apartment, compared to all our living situations over the years.

Carol was twenty-three years old and married to Jeff. They lived in a trailer park with their two kids, a toddler and a baby who wasn't even sitting up yet. When she and Jeff started to have problems in their marriage, she and the kids moved in with us. Since I didn't have my own bed, Carol and the kids took my room.

I was excited about Carol living with us. For once we could "be there for her" in a way that I knew my mother had never been able to be. I had stayed with Carol and Jeff in the trailer for a couple of nights two or three years earlier. This was a few months after we'd shown up in Columbus from Phoenix. A few months after Carol's mother blew in from somewhere after a fifteen-year absence, with a new kid in tow. She was nice to me then. Plus, she cooked.

Carol qualified for government assistance, and, unlike Chlotene, she used it. She got food delivered through WIC.[1] She was organized enough to show up for her appointments and receive her benefits, something Chlotene would never do. Pride, paranoia, and disorganization kept Chlotene from them, but Carol didn't have those hang-ups.

She had appointments to keep with the Welfare Department. She went to the pantry. She smoked, and from time to time, she would tell me to run down to the gas station to get her cigarettes. She'd give me money and a handwritten note and tell me to cross at the light, an admonishment that must have been a force of habit for the mom of a toddler.

We didn't have a television at the time, so the radio was on from morning to night. I was thirteen and always wanted to listen to Top 40. This was 1983, the year of "Billie Jean" and "Beat It." She wanted soft rock. We bickered, but for the most part, I stayed on my best behavior. I wanted us to get along.

Soon after she moved in with her kids, we all moved out to a poor white neighborhood on the south side of Columbus.

The house was just around the corner from Maybeline's house. Maybeline was my half-brother John's mother-in-law. Even though we weren't related by blood and weren't really closely related at all, I found myself at Maybeline's house often. She watched out for John's whole clan, and that included Chlotene and me. She fed me. Taught me how to make cornbread in a skillet. She lent me a bike, which I rode all summer. She was a force that brought people together.

She even gave my mom an old refrigerator, without which we would have had no refrigerated food for our few months in that house. That's how my mom rolled. No refrigerator? Why would we need a refrigerator? We could do without.

The fridge was so old that it required weekly defrosting or it would accumulate so much ice that it became unusable.

Did Carol encourage the move? Did she have a conversation with Chlo about how moving there would be more convenient for her? I don't know. One summer day I got home from playing outside with the other kids in the apartment complex, and Chlotene told me we'd be moving into a house the next day.

Loxley Avenue had houses with chain-link fenced yards, couches on front porches, and multiple cars up on blocks in driveways and parked on the street. Our house was tucked into the part of the street that bottomed out to a dead-end of trees and weeds that covered a creek. If the house had been in a nicer neighborhood, you could have called it a tucked-away gem with privacy. It was the very last house on the street. But in this neighborhood, it felt isolated and creepy, especially at night.

Chlotene wasn't equipped to move us into a house. Apartments come with a lot of things built in. Fridge. Stove. Groundskeeping. Repairs. Trash bins. We had never needed to purchase a bin for trash pickup. She wasn't ready for all those expenses. They hadn't even occurred to her.

The outside of the house was painted orange. Well, most of the house was painted orange. Someone decided to quit about three-quarters of the way through. So three-quarters orange and one-quarter unpainted white.

There was a cement porch and a large picture window at the end of the driveway. A fellow church member, Robert, owned the place. He wore a toupee. He came by a few times to mow the lawn, although he ended each visit by saying he couldn't keep doing that, hoping he could shame her into finding someone else.

I was taken away from any friends I had, for the most

part. Not that I wasn't happy. This was the first time I had ever lived in an actual house in a residential neighborhood, and that felt big. But having Carol and her kids with us took some of the sting out of leaving the apartment complex in Whitehall and the friends I'd made there. We were finally making a go of it as a family.

Jeff, Carol's husband, would come by every now and then to pick up the kids or take Carol and them out for dinner.

One summer night, Jeff drove up in his boat of a car. He pulled into our gravel and dirt driveway. As Carol left the house, Chlotene sprinted out after her and screamed at her and Jeff in the street.

"DON'T YOU GO WITH HIM! IF YOU GO WITH HIM, DON'T YOU EVER COME BACK HERE!"

I was mortified. Chlotene was acting crazy again.

Carol was answering, "I won't come back! I'll be back to get my stuff, and *you won't see me ever again!*"

As I was watching this happen from the porch, I was shaking and crying. What was wrong with her? Why was she starting a fight about nothing? Why was she starting a fight with the only sibling of mine who wanted to spend time with us?

"Stop it. *STOP IT!*" I shouted. "Shut up! If you don't talk, people won't know you're this way!" She was so humiliating. "Stop it! *I hate you!* You're ruining my life!" I kept screaming at her from the porch. But neither she nor Carol paid any attention to me. They were too busy screaming at each other.

Carol got in the car, and they peeled off down the street.

I have not seen Carol since.

I think back on that fight, think back on me yelling from the porch, and I know these fights weren't normal fights, not even "normal" fights for abusive people or people with anger issues. In a "normal fight"—even a heated or drunken one—

some kind of escalation happens. Both people who are in the fight have a sense of what's going on. Someone says something mean or offensive, and then there's a retort that's meaner. Then yelling. Then maybe hitting or something like that. A bit like going from zero to sixty in three seconds. The escalation might follow a steep slope, but it's still *a slope*.

Chlotene's confrontations had the notable absence of all that. She didn't escalate. She started at towering tsunami. If you could see the tsunami, it was already too late. Just like when she stuck a finger in the face of one of my childhood playmates when I was five or six. Just like when she threw Joan out of the apartment.

Her paranoia made her see things that terrified her. She wasn't just angry when she yelled. She was frightened too. She was so certain that she was justified in her rage that she felt abandoned by the reactions of others. The sane reactions. The looks on people's faces.

Nobody jumped on her bandwagon. She was alone.

———

Now we lived in this house on Loxley Avenue, alone again, and far from my friends. I didn't want to start a new school. I had heard bad things about the junior high school in this neighborhood, and I was worried I'd get beat up and terrorized.

"We need to go back to Whitehall," I told her. I prodded her to find us a new place, and we picked up and moved, twice, until we were back in the apartment complex where we'd been. It took a few months, and it meant that I had to start eighth grade late, but it was the best I could do to introduce some sort of safety back into my life. At least I was back at the junior high where I'd finished out seventh grade, the place where I'd been before Carol came. I gave myself that stability.

When I joined the eighth-grade class, the teacher introduced me as a new student.

"She's not new," one of the kids blurted out.

"Yeah, I went here last year," I said.

When we got back to Whitehall and I felt safer again at school (although I was still bullied), I started to hate my mom. I felt trapped. By this time, I had a lot of independence as a young teenager. I was spending as much time as possible with my two friends, especially friends from church. I was glad that they hadn't forgotten about me over the summer while I was living on the other side of town. Whenever I visited their homes and their families, I saw I could have a different life. Other people had a different life! Why not me? I wanted to escape her as much as I could. I even switched churches so I wouldn't have to spend Sundays with her.

She stayed at our old church, but I was spared from cringing every time she opened her mouth, or every time she got up in front of the whole congregation, pressed PLAY on a tape, and started to sing. She couldn't sing, of course. That didn't stop her from singing at least one solo, sometimes more, in her totally off-key voice.

She did that almost every Sunday until the pastor pulled her aside privately after a service and told her the church was going in a different direction with its musical lineup.

His decision made no sense to her. Why would they keep her from singing on Sundays?

PART II

"*But I promise that I'll take special pains today so you won't have to be ashamed of me.*"[1]

4

I FOUND this letter among Chlotene's things in the summer of 2020. It's from Theresa, Chlotene's oldest child, who was born in 1959. Chlo was nineteen.

It's dated 1984, so I was fourteen. Theresa would have only been twenty-five herself when she wrote it. Married with a six-year-old daughter and one-year-old son.

In neat cursive, she writes:

Dear Mother & Em,

Just a quick note before I go to bed. Been real busy today. Worked until lunch. Then cleaned entire house. Made dinner, did dishes, made oatmeal cookies, then spent two to three hours at the sewing machine repairing the kids' clothes. Got some of the closets cleaned too. Got a big pile for the Goodwill. This apartment is too small for anything but the barest of essentials! Oh well.

Sorry I haven't been up to date on my letter writing . . . Seems like I'm always busy even though there's not much to do. But never enough time to do what I want.

Jennifer is doing real well in school. Did you know she was a

> *munchkin in the Wizard of Oz at the Cambridge Theater of Performing Arts? I took her to try out 'cause it's her favorite movie, and I thought it might be fun. She got the part and really enjoyed it. We are now all sick of the Wizard, and if I ever hear "Ding Dong the Witch is Dead" again, I'll probably scream.*

She continues with updates about her kids and a recent family camping trip. Then she says:

> *... I gotta close. I'm too tired to write another word.*
> *Theresa, Bob, and the kids.*
> *Jennifer just got her school pictures taken, so as soon as I get them, I'll send one.*
> *P.S.: [Written in print and with a different pen] Sorry about condition of this letter. Brendan got ahold of it. His way of saying, "Hi!"*

I held the letter in my hands and read it again. I've always thought Chlotene's four older kids wanted nothing to do with her. But when I read the letter, I see that what her kids really wanted has always been a lot less definitive—and more complicated—than that.

The inarguable fact: Chlotene is the one who left them behind. Not the other way around.

Another fact, which probably seemed a lot more arguable at the time: she was too sick to seek help, too sick to have the insight that she might need help, and so she remained too sick to take care of them. So she abandoned them. By the time she returned to Ohio in 1979 with a nine-year-old daughter and an unexplained fifteen-year absence, they had learned to live without her. Yet they had not moved on totally, at least not Theresa. Otherwise, why would she write?

The adults around them didn't attribute Chlotene's behavior to schizophrenia or to any other mental illness. Her behavior was attributed to a character flaw called "being nuts."

If they were getting information about their mother from their dad, Eric, then here's how they understood their mom's decision: When Chlotene voluntarily gave up the family home and full custody of the kids, they went to court to formalize the new arrangement. Eric insisted on a token child support payment from her of five dollars a week.

"I have yet to see a single five-dollar bill," he told me. "She just wanted to go live a different life." He waved his hand in dismissal of all that. As if waving a hand could wave away the memory.

And even when her kids reached out, like Theresa did in this letter, Chlotene was just too sick to see it, to acknowledge or respond.

Whenever I saw them, which wasn't often, they kept their distance. I still remember the first time I met them back in 1979. My daydreams of warmly connecting with long-lost siblings never materialized. Unsurprising to me now as an adult, but as a nine-year-old, I was bitterly disappointed.

A whole family had appeared—dad, siblings, cousins, an aunt and uncle—but they weren't the insta-family I'd assumed I would get.

My half-siblings must have felt a lot of anger about their mom disappearing, but they had nowhere to direct it. Their father had a girlfriend by the time we moved back to Columbus. He'd moved on.

They were left to contend with the stigma of mental illness, a stigma that wasn't just within our family but was the widely accepted way to deal with mental illness in the early 1980s. They knew Chlo was "not right," but they didn't ever utter the word "schizophrenia" or wonder (aloud, at least) why she wasn't receiving treatment.

They, in turn, would call her "nuts" as they reached adulthood. Just like the adults around them did. I never overheard any conversation like this. If I had, it would have been helpful. It would have validated my own experience. But my half-sister Michelle told me about conversations she'd had with Chlotene's other kids. She said they had talked about her delusions in a "Can you believe this?" tone. When they talked about her at all.

I first met Michelle in 1998 when I was twenty-eight. She was twenty-nine, and she looked so much like Chlo that it freaked me out a little. She had the same long, lanky black hair that Chlo had on our Greyhound bus ride from Phoenix to Columbus. She laughed like Chlotene (and like me). When I first heard her laugh, I felt like I was in one of those movies where two strangers meet by chance on an airplane and realize they're sisters when they both pull the same snack out of their purses or something like that.

She's got the same round face, same nose and nasolabial folds and thin lips. Chlotene delivered Michelle in Columbus in February 1969, fourteen months before I was born in Phoenix. Michelle was adopted as a newborn in a closed adoption in Ohio. Chlo moved to Phoenix two weeks later.

Like me, Michelle has no idea who her biological father is. But after her adoptive parents died, she set her mind on fulfilling a lifelong wish to find Chlotene. She hired a private investigator and soon got in touch.

She met us all over the next few months. When she was with my mother's kids from Chlo's first marriage, they talked about what a nut Chlotene was. How Chlotene claimed to have called the FBI to leave a tip about Timothy McVeigh's plot to bomb the federal building in Oklahoma City. That Chlotene said she used to live next door to Ted Kaczynski, the Unabomber. And so on.

Once, years later, I had a party at my house, and Michelle was there. We could both overhear Chlotene talking to someone she didn't know at the party. She was unspooling a delusion about meeting Osama bin Laden at a nursing home where she worked. Chlotene never ranted or raved when she delivered her delusions. In fact, her delusions weren't stories she told. It was more like her delusions coated her conversation. She might drop a hint of a delusion into polite conversation. In this case, the stranger, not knowing anything about Chlotene, started to ask more questions. "When was this?" and "Did you tell anyone else?"

Michelle began to laugh hysterically as she listened to their conversation. I rarely heard my mother laugh heartily, but when she did, she sounded just like Michelle.

5

As I neared high school graduation in the late spring of 1988, I was arranging to move out. Getting my own place had been the ultimate goal of my teen years, and maybe the ultimate goal of my entire childhood. I was working, and I had a modest amount of money saved. So I rented an apartment. I put down the deposit. I signed the lease.

I told Chlotene about it. "I got my own place, mom. It's about a mile from here."

"Uh-huh," she said. "OK."

I started to pack boxes, and Tim, who was my boyfriend at the time, helped me load his car for the move. And it hit her. I was moving.

"If you move out, I'm not gonna let you come back," she said, as if that would make me say, *Oh. Really? In that case, I guess I change my mind. I'll stay forever.*

———

The tighter Chlotene held on to me, the more I knew I wanted to get away from her. As I hit adolescence in the early 1980s, a lot of my life was me waiting to turn eighteen and graduate.

In seventh grade, I insisted I get a bed of my own. I had slept in the same full-size bed with Chlotene my entire life. We didn't have money for a second bed, I knew that. And Chlotene's habit of leaving behind anything that she couldn't carry whenever we moved meant that we had almost no furniture.

But I knew we could have gotten another bed from Goodwill or a church. I needed a bed of my own, and I told her so. I wasn't willing to sleep in the same bed with her anymore. So our church gave us a twin-size ottoman, which was the closest I ever got to having my own bed under Chlotene's roof. (I didn't get a bed with a mattress until I moved out at eighteen. I bought a terrible ninety-nine-dollar frame and mattress, but it was a big moment for me. I felt like a real adult capable of shopping for, and paying for, my own furniture.)

The ottoman wasn't exactly a bed, but it was better than the floor. Once I got the ottoman, Chlotene still insisted that I wasn't allowed to keep my bedroom door closed. She couldn't trust me, and by this time I was the target of all sorts of paranoid delusions that involved me "wanting to get raped," "trying to have sex," and "touching myself."

Her paranoia ran circles in her brain. I started to see her as very fucked up, but I wasn't even close to knowing what the term "mentally ill" meant.

I just hated her. Another "natural" part of being a teen for most kids. But not, because of Chlotene's illness.

"I'm going to shut my door if I want to. You're being crazy!" I screamed at her. "All my friends are allowed to close their door when they want!"

I knew even as I was "rebelling" like a teenager that I was the grown-up in the situation, too, demanding a boundary. I was demanding that she at least *tolerate* my perception of reality, even if she couldn't see the reality that I saw.

She was demanding that I do the same, and I did just as much as I needed to so that I could live under her roof.

I met Tim in 1986 when I was sixteen and he was nineteen. We were both working at the Drug Emporium. I was making $3.33 as a cashier. He wasn't my first boyfriend; I'd already been dating someone else, another employee. But that guy dumped me when he quit the job. I developed a crush on Tim because he was older—already in college when I met him. And I thought he was cute.

We started dating when I was seventeen. On some level, I was looking for someone to take care of me. I had been looking for someone to take care of me for all of my short life. I'm not sure I believed that Tim could be that person, but I was making plans to get out on my own, no matter what happened with Tim.

When I was thirteen, one of the neighborhood girls showed me her hope chest. She told me it was a place to save sheets, towels, and dishes. Things you would need when you got married, she said. So I started my own hope chest when I got my first job. When I had money, I would go to the ninety-nine cents store and buy dishes. Towels. Sheets. And put them in my hope chest. I used all those things in my first apartment. My hope chest was the reason I had anything to move with me at all at eighteen.

By my senior year, I had a job at a bank, and I knew I could move out as soon as I graduated. I didn't join clubs in high school. I didn't care about sports or school spirit or even doing *well* in school. I just wanted to pass so I could get my diploma. I focused on graduating high school and moving out like they were the pinnacle of what was possible for my life. I didn't have a plan for what I would do once I achieved those two goals because it felt far from certain that I would ever graduate or leave Chlotene.

She'd been paranoid my whole life that "the system" or some other named or unnamed paranoid hallucination would separate me from her. Any number of what seemed to her like totally reasonable possibilities. She had no ability to understand that I might move out.

Well, it's not entirely true that I didn't have a plan for what I would do once I graduated and moved out. I had been making promises to myself ever since the day I had asked Chlotene if I should wear underwear with my baptismal gown and she had screamed at me about wanting to get raped.

One of my promises to myself was that I'd get my own bed to replace that dreadful ottoman I was sleeping on. Another promise to myself: "When I have money and a job, and I don't have to take care of my mom anymore, I'm going to eat pizza whenever I want." To this day, I could eat pizza twice a week.

One evening early in our relationship, I went to Tim's dad and stepmom's house for Sunday dinner. They had family dinner together every Sunday, with a revolving group of their grown kids, spouses, and families.

I had only known Tim for a few months, and I doubt it occurred to him that he might need to prep me in any way for a family dinner. He didn't know, for example, that I'd never been to a house for dinner where the table was set—linen tablecloth and all— before we sat down to eat.

The plates and forks and spoons were neatly laid out,

water and wine glasses were sitting up and to the right of each place setting, empty and sparkling. I was about to embark on something totally new to me, and I didn't want to embarrass myself.

If we ate dinner at all when I was growing up, Chlotene and I didn't eat at the same time. We didn't eat at a dining table, that's for sure, let alone a dining table that was set. I usually ate on the floor in front of the TV (that is, the times when we had a TV).

Maureen, Tim's stepmom, called us in for dinner. I remember not understanding what all the silverware was for. So I watched what the other people at the table did, what Tim did.

They put their napkins in their laps, so I did too.

They used the small fork to eat their salad, so I did too.

They asked someone to pass the salt instead of reaching across the table. Not only did I not grow up asking anyone to pass anything, but I didn't even grow up with a salt or pepper shaker in the house. But I caught on and asked Tim to please pass me the salt too.

I'd also grown up eating a lot more things with my spoon than Tim's family seemed to. Lima beans, peas, mashed potatoes—that's what a spoon was for in our house. So the one detail I missed was how they ate their peas by pushing them onto their forks with their knives. Without thinking, I ate my peas with the teaspoon that had been set out at my place, above my dinner plate, perpendicular to the other silverware.

When it was time for dessert, Tim's stepmom, Maureen, got up from the table and nonchalantly replaced my teaspoon with a new one. I was the only person she'd done that for. As she served coffee with dessert, I noted that the others used their spoons to stir their coffee. I never ate peas with a teaspoon again.

My first apartment had a red shag carpet with radiator heating and crank-out windows. It was $270 a month plus utilities. I had a full-time job working for a bank. I was exhausted, and after a few months, I wanted to escape again. Moving in together without getting married would have scandalized both our families. I wanted something that felt like a sure thing, that felt easy and right.

I proposed to Tim. I guess you could say I "proposed," if telling him I wanted to get married and threatening to break up with him if we didn't get married counts as a "proposal." Romantic, huh? We were married in February 1990, a couple of months before I turned twenty.

After we got married, I converted to Catholicism and threw myself into joining Tim's family. They seemed so normal and so *middle class*. They seemed to live a predictable life that I found intensely appealing. And they had each other. They bantered and joked playfully when they were together. They didn't seem to be keeping any secrets.

In Tim's family, Tim and his siblings were all expected to go to college. I wanted to fit in with his family, so I enrolled at Ohio State University the week after I graduated high school. I had never even considered college. In my senior year of high school, I was in a secretarial program for women who weren't going anywhere near college.

When I mentioned I wanted to try college, my typing teacher told me I didn't have what it took to get through college and told me to focus on getting a job. Specifically, a job as an assistant to an executive whom I could follow up a ladder of promotions. As his assistant, his promotions would become mine. The conversation pissed me off and solidified my decision to go to college. Even then, I knew I could do better than hitch a ride on someone else's success. But, with my GPA, I knew I wouldn't be accepted into Ohio State if I applied for the fall semester. At that time Ohio State had open enrollment during the summer. So I was accepted on the condition that I test out of remedial math and English courses. I passed the tests and was allowed to stay enrolled.

I worked at a variety of full-time and part-time jobs while I was in school, including the bank, Pizza Hut, Wendy's, and as a server at a restaurant in a country club. Tim lived with his parents while he was in college all the way up until the day we got married. He graduated from college the quarter after I started college. He continued working at Drug Emporium as a stocker and helped them open their new store. I think about it now . . . he had no ambition. Before we got married, he accepted the first full-time job he was offered. It was in a call center making just under seven dollars an hour, which was peanuts even back then. But, based upon my history, this seemed normal to me.

I was married, in school, working, and very busy. Tim's family was an island of safety after treading water my entire childhood in shark-infested waters. And then the island crumbled and washed back out into the same sea I had just escaped.

Years after I met my sister Michelle and we became pretty friendly, she once described Tim as "a flat line." From the outside, I can see how someone might see him that way. He was never a reactive or outwardly emotional person.

His placidity was something I liked about him, especially when we first met. He never exploded at me the way

Chlotene did. He wouldn't have known how to. I took this gentleness for granted after a couple of years, but at first it refreshed me to know that I could fly off the handle and Tim would never shout me down or hit me.

But "flat line" also hints at stability and security. We didn't have those things during our marriage. Certainly not financial stability. After Tim graduated college, he kept the call center job for years. Even when he was promoted, he was still grossly underpaid. We had two preschool children and were charging food and diapers to a credit card. I insisted that he ask for a ten-thousand-dollar raise or threaten to resign, and he actually did it. His annual salary went from twenty thousand to thirty thousand—a 33 percent increase.

A flat line makes me think of predictability too. But we didn't have that either. The issues in our marriage were deep, and they joined us from the very beginning.

"I don't think I want kids," I told him. We had married in February and had this conversation in March. As a nineteen-year-old, it hadn't occurred to me to make sure we were on the same page about kids before our wedding.

He nodded. I saw what I wanted to see, and what I wanted to see was him wholeheartedly agreeing with me. No kids. The two of us on the same page.

Now I see that he wasn't agreeing, exactly. He was just doing the thing he did when he was my boyfriend.

"What do you want to do Friday night?" I might say. Or, "You want to stop for burgers, or should we just get hot dogs at the bowling alley?"

And he would say, "Whatever you want to do."

Let's just do whatever you want to do.

It seemed he had no opinion. I got used to him saying that. I started to expect it. Maybe once in a while it got slightly annoying. A little voice in my head might pipe up, "Why doesn't he decide?" But it seemed silly to be annoyed, especially at nineteen years old. I should be more than happy with that answer, shouldn't I?

"*Whatever I want? Works for me!*"

I always had an opinion. I always had a preference. And I always got my way.

We continued talking about how we didn't want to have kids. Or how I didn't want to have kids and how he wanted to do what I wanted to do. A few weeks later, I made him an appointment for a vasectomy. I didn't see the fact that *I* was making the appointment as a red flag. He went in for a pre-procedure consultation, and I went with him.

We sat down next to each other, and the doctor took his seat on the other side of his messy wooden desk. The first thing the doctor said to Tim was, "You're pretty young to be making this decision. Are you sure you really want to do this?"

I inhaled, set my jaw, and stared blankly at the wall just above the doctor's head, into the space between the doctor's question and his response.

Tim inhaled too. "Well, I don't know," he exhaled. "I'm not sure."

I felt my heart seize in my chest and my face turn red-hot before I could exhale.

I looked at Tim. Flabbergasted. "Are you kidding me?"

I looked at the doctor. "You know this is not the order of things, right? People have this conversation before ever coming into your office. This is not the conversation we had."

I wanted the doctor to have my back, but he didn't. They both just stared blankly.

Turning back to Tim: "Why am I just now hearing this is

how you feel? In front of this stranger? How did we get all the way here if you weren't sure?" I said.

Tim mumbled an apology. I felt disgusted. They were both afraid of me, staring past the top of my head at the white walls of the office. I stood up and said, "Let's leave."

The doctor urged Tim to think about it. I nodded in a white-hot rage, storming out the door ahead of Tim so he wouldn't touch me.

I felt like a fool. Suddenly I was in a position where I seemed to be forcing him to have a vasectomy. I thought he didn't want kids. But the truth was that he didn't know how to tell me he did want them. I thought we had talked about it.

On the ride from the appointment to our apartment, I transferred some of my anger to the doctor. "What a question to ask! Why would he just blurt out a question like that?"

When we got home from the doctor's office, I carried on for a while. Eventually, we agreed not to worry about kids "for now." I felt humiliated because, on some level, I'd known all along. My shame made me not want to talk about what had happened. I felt like I had stepped in it. Like I'd been a ball-buster. So I dropped the whole conversation, and Tim didn't bring it up either.

But from then on, I was never sure I could trust Tim. I knew I couldn't trust him to even know himself or what he wanted. About a year and a half later, I was pregnant with my first baby.

In the meantime, in 1990 and '91, we had no kids, but I was still struggling to work and go to school full-time. I had been in school for three and a half years, and I had just one semester to go when Chlotene called me.

She'd quit her job. It was the best job she'd ever had working at AT&T. She'd stayed there for five years, a huge accomplishment for Chlotene, and the longest she'd ever held down any job.

"They just don't like me there anymore, Emily," she said in her naive, credulous voice. "They wanted to fire me—they were just trying to figure out the best way to do it."

"Well, why didn't you wait until they actually fired you instead of quitting first?"

"It was too far to drive. I'm not sure my car can keep making it over there every day."

She just changed the reason. I was exasperated but very used to this switcheroo. The paranoid delusion that was compelling her to quit coated the conversation instead of being the focus of it.

That was why if I questioned her reason, instead of insisting on what she'd just said, she'd feel free to just pluck a new reason from thin air. The reason was never what she said out loud but whatever stayed between her ears, unvoiced, no matter how disorganized.

Six years later, in 1998, I was working toward a master's degree in social work and studying psychiatric disorders. I read:

> The person may "slip off the track" from one topic to another ("derailment" or "loose associations"); answers to questions may be obliquely related or completely unrelated (tangentiality) . . . Because mildly disorganized speech is common and nonspecific, the symptom must be severe enough to impair effective communication.[1]

But in 1991 I didn't know any of that. I just knew that she

made no sense and that was the story of her life. At the time that made it the story of my life too.

She soon sold her car for almost nothing and asked me for money because she couldn't cover her mortgage payment. We didn't have much, but I scraped together a couple hundred dollars for her. I knew that wouldn't be enough and that she'd need more if she was going to keep her house.

Her chaos was my chaos; her problems were my problems. The crisis as I defined it at the time: *"My mom is going to lose her house."*

As a twenty-one-year-old newlywed, I was both highly emotionally wrapped up in what Chlotene was doing with herself and had almost no insight about the limits to what I could do about it. I defined her problems as situational, and that made them seem like things I could control. Money, food, shelter. But her problems were not those things.

In any case, I knew that I did not ever want her to live with us. I had lived away from Chlotene for just one year, and the very last thing I wanted was for her to move in with us. So I believed I needed to get more work so I could start supporting her. At the time, I was waiting tables, and Tim and I lived in a one-bedroom apartment.

I was losing interest in school, too, especially as I was getting closer to finishing. I couldn't see the point in getting my degree. Maybe my typing teacher was right. Maybe I wasn't cut out for college and I would never make it.

I started reminding myself that I'd never had a lot of drive to go to college in the first place, that it was Tim's family that had made me feel like I should give it a try. That I was an English major because Tim had been an English major. That my grades were dipping. That my mom needed money. That I couldn't "let her" lose the house. I decided to drop out.

But once I quit school and started working full-time, Chlotene called the bank, told them she was about to default on her mortgage, and moved out. She hadn't even missed a single payment yet. She just called to tell them that she had made her last payment and she wouldn't be making any more.

I asked her, "Why not just wait until they kick you out?" But she couldn't find the words to answer me.

By then, I was working at places like Wendy's and as a phone rep for Victoria's Secret Catalogue. Jobs that felt like dead ends. I was letting go of any vision I had for my life, for wealth, for becoming great at something. Tim wanted to continue going to work every day, to come home, to play golf with his dad on the weekends. He had the life he wanted. I was losing the thread that connected me to what I wanted. I was running out of gas.

Tim and I decided to get pregnant the same way we had decided earlier not to have kids. It was my idea.

I brought it up because having kids seemed like that next thing—something exciting that we could bring to our relationship. Something we could have, something that didn't involve travel or taking a huge risk or anything like the other things in which Tim showed no interest.

Tim expressed some doubts at first. He thought we might not be ready financially. (We weren't.) But I countered that no one ever feels really ready. Once I pushed back, he relented right away.

Let's do what you want to do.

We had our first baby, Barbara, in 1992. I got pregnant with our second baby, Rachel, in 1994. Eight months into that pregnancy, Tim sat me down and told me about the sexual abuse he had suffered as a child.

I was twenty-three by now. We'd been married four years. The priest that married us was Phil Jacobs. Jacobs was also the priest who molested Tim.

When Tim was telling me, "I think I might have been sexually abused by Father Jacobs," he was so unsure about whether it really even happened. He wasn't sure if he "made it happen." Or maybe, he even wondered aloud, if he wasn't just overreacting to harmless "fun."

My response in that conversation was, "We have to tell people." I knew from the moment he told me that he was abused. I believed him, even if he didn't know whether to believe his own memories.

"What if there are other people? What if one of your brothers was abused? Or your friends?"

But he also shifted in my eyes at that moment into a victim whom I had to take care of. Chlotene was often a victim when I was growing up. A victim of her own paranoid delusions. A victim of very real things that happened to her, like when all her money was stolen or we got stranded far from home because the bus we were waiting for never showed up.

So I'd had experiences taking care of a victim. When it came to Chlo, it meant I needed to take care of things, manage things. Remind her about overdue bills. Rearrange furniture. And when I was older, insist she stop bringing strangers home to live with us. I handled many things that she should have handled.

In the moment when Tim told me about the abuse, I made a complete shift, whether it was deserved or not. I no longer had trust in his competence as a spouse, husband, life partner. I couldn't trust him anymore. Throughout our marriage he was always there for me, but I wasn't able to see it. All I saw was a victim.

I stopped believing I could count on him from that moment forward. He took on a different image of who I thought he was. Cemented by his passivity. He didn't take the lead in going after Phil Jacobs, and that never sat right with me.

6

AFTER TIM TOLD me about the abuse, I was *into action*. Amped up. "We have to tell the diocese! We have to make an appointment with the Columbus diocese right away!"

We went to the diocese. We didn't make Tim's story a public issue until several years later, after we found out the church didn't do the right thing. One day Father Jacobs just disappeared. When I found out that he was moved to a diocese in Canada and continued working with children, that's when we took it to the press.

But the echoes of the abuse—the impact it had had on Tim and on our marriage and family by extension—were not really fixable. I was busy trying to expose Jacobs, but even as I led the charge to do that, we were still left with the fact that it had happened.

So Tim wasn't the person I thought he was. But it wasn't OK for me to say that because it wasn't OK for me to think that. Tim didn't feel the need to go to therapy. I started therapy. I demanded that it be paid for by the Columbus diocese, which they did for nearly five years.

In therapy I decided I would go back to school. I had this fantasy of what it meant to be a therapist. I read *The Road Less Traveled*. *I could save people!* I thought. Something I'd always wanted to do for my mom but never had any luck with.

Tim wasn't going to be able to take care of me. I needed to figure out a way to take care of us.

After his revelation and all I had been through with Chlotene, I did what a lot of people do when they haven't processed their trauma: I decided I wanted to help *other* people.

I also realized, after working so many low-paying, dead-end jobs, that I wanted to be a professional with a stable career that paid better than what we had at that time.

I decided that I wanted to be a psychotherapist and open a private practice. So I went back to school and earned my bachelor's degree in social work at Ohio Dominican College. Then I immediately began my master's in social work at Ohio State.

The massive student loans I took out to pay for college felt at the time like a financial life preserver when we sorely needed one. They paid for childcare for my two daughters, who were only four and two when I started my master's program.

The loans paid for so many expenses that we wouldn't have been able to cover otherwise. We had been kiting checks just to pay for things like diapers and groceries, and we were always in credit card debt. In fact, we used our credit limit like a bank balance. The loans reduced that daily financial stress, and they meant I didn't have to work full-time, so I could focus on school.

This time, with a clear sense of purpose, I did focus. At Ohio Dominican, I earned good grades. Earning my MSW would allow me to get licensed as a psychotherapist, a clear goal I was intent on pursuing.

I remember at this time taking a Clinical Diagnosis class to learn how to assess and diagnose mental illness. I'd gotten my bachelor's in social work, and I was well into my master's program, but up until then, studying for these degrees had involved learning about the history of social work, community and grassroots organizing, and how to broker services, like connecting people who needed housing or food to the right resources.

Clinical Diagnosis was one of the first classes I'd taken that specifically focused on mental health. We studied the *Diagnostic and Statistical Manual of Mental Disorders, Fourth Edition*, known as the DSM-IV, which is the bible of psychiatric diagnosis and is thicker than the actual Bible.

I remember working through the book at home, flipping through the sections.

Delirium, Dementia, and Amnestic and Other Cognitive Disorders. Mental Disorders Due to a General Medical Condition. Substance-Related Disorders. Schizophrenia and Other Psychotic Disorders. Mood Disorders. Anxiety Disorders.

And so on.

At this point, I was nearly thirty. I hadn't lived with Chlotene for over a decade. As a kid growing up, I'd never even heard of a social worker, let alone come into contact with one. Now I was learning that this entire profession was designed to help people like the kid I'd been.

I wasn't that kid anymore. I had achieved my childhood ambition of getting away from Chlotene. But my internships had me working with severely mentally ill people living in poverty. I worked with homeless families and with single moms who abused and neglected their children. I saw Chlotene in them, and myself in their children.

A thought was working its way to the surface of my brain.

I read through the "Differential Diagnosis" subsection in the schizophrenia category:

> The differential diagnosis between schizophrenia and delusional disorder rests on the nature of the delusions (nonbizarre in delusional disorder) and the absence of other characteristic symptoms of schizophrenia (e.g., hallucinations, disorganized speech or behavior, or prominent negative symptoms).[1]

I moved to the diagnostic criteria for schizophrenia, a kind of checklist.

1. Characteristic symptoms: Two (or more) of the following, each present for a significant portion of time during a 1-month period (or less if successfully treated):
2. delusions
3. hallucinations
4. disorganized speech (e.g., frequent derailment or incoherence)
5. grossly disorganized or catatonic behavior
6. negative symptoms, i.e., affective flattening, alogia, or avolition

Note: Only 1 Criterion A symptom is required if delusions are bizarre or hallucinations consist of a voice keeping up a running commentary on the person's behavior or thoughts, or two or more voices conversing with each other.[2]

I turned the page and skimmed the subheading "295.30—Paranoid Type."

A type of schizophrenia in which the following criteria are met:

1. Preoccupation with one or more delusions or frequent auditory hallucinations.[3]

I was fifteen. I had just gotten home from my Drug Emporium job.

"If anyone asks you to get into a car with them, say no," she told me anxiously. "You make sure you say no!"

"What are you talking about?" I asked. "Did you see someone?"

"I just saw your father drive by."

I was intrigued. My father? She'd always told me that he had never had any interest in us. In me. He left my mom high and dry as soon as he found out she was pregnant. That was her story.

"Are you sure it was him?" I asked.

"He always drives a white Cadillac," she said.

"Did you talk to him?" I asked.

But she just repeated her worry. "If anyone asks you to get into a car with them, don't do it."

She was "acting crazy" again. I'd thrown the ball, and she'd tossed back a raw egg, and I stiffened, contorting myself, to catch it gingerly without breaking it.

"Mom," I said, "If my dad comes by, that doesn't mean I'll move in with him or something. I don't even know him."

I told her that again when she "saw" him drive by a few months later. And again a month after that. I always brought the same level of indignation to my performance.

"Come on, Mom! Why would I leave you?"

I felt that reassuring her was my job, a feeling reinforced by the fact that she would calm down when I reassured her.

She would stop. She would scrounge up ten dollars and make a stack of peanut butter sandwiches so that we wouldn't starve.

She would get it together for a while.

I knew she was "acting crazy" back then, at fifteen. But now I had words to put to it.

Delusion. Paranoid.

Diagnostic criteria for schizophrenia:

1. *Social/occupational dysfunction:* For a significant portion of the time since the onset of the disturbance, one or more major areas of functioning such as work, interpersonal relations, or self-care are markedly below the level achieved prior to the onset (or when the onset is in childhood or adolescence, failure to achieve expected level of interpersonal, academic, or occupational achievement).[4]

I thought about all the times she'd quit a job without having another lined up. All the times she'd moved us out of an apartment without any place to go. How she'd left four of her children in Ohio without a word and disappeared to Phoenix for ten years.

. . . when the onset is in . . . adolescence, **failure to achieve expected level of interpersonal, academic, or occupational achievement.**

Curious. I felt curious as I studied the book. But lightning wasn't striking me.

By the time I was paging through that DSM-IV, studying for my master's degree, I didn't want to dive back into that past by mulling over whether I could get help for Chlotene. She wouldn't have accepted help if I'd tried.

Even as a teenager when I lived with her, how could I have gotten my mom help, even if I knew "help" existed, and even if she could have accepted it?

Attempting to get her help would have been like exploding a grenade in the middle of my life. I don't know where I would have gone or whether staying with other family members (even if they could have or would have agreed to take me in) would have been a better situation. As her child, I was stuck with her until I figured out a way to move out right after high school.

And now, twelve years later as a thirty-year-old, not much had changed, at least when it came to what she could have gained from seeking help. She was high-functioning, living on her own, holding down a job for the most part, much better than the kind of jobs she'd had in Phoenix. She worked in offices as an assistant, and she also worked as a home health aide. She still shuffled through jobs quite often, but she lived alone and seemed able to make rent. She eventually got her medical assistant certification.

What would "help" have looked like for her in this period of her life? Years of experimenting with types and dosages of drugs, with side effects that might have made it impossible for her to work?

Did she need treatment? How could she decide that for herself when she had no insight into the fact that she had a mental illness?

Life was an Etch A Sketch. At first she was able to navigate, to draw in straight lines. But the curves got messy, the surface got so cluttered, and every time she tried to fix it, it just got worse until there was nothing to do but shake it up and start over. She moved on to the next apartment, the next job, the next church. She left people, places, and things behind and found a sort of temporary solace in the blank canvas.

The people who remained in her life long enough to see that she was more than "eccentric" were always the ones who minimized, miscategorized, and ignored her behavior. Even those people have their limits.

Her fellow churchgoers tolerated her. Even the one who whispered in my ear, "There's something wrong with your mom."

The gulf between whispers about Chlotene's eccentric behavior and words like "mental health treatment" and "schizophrenia" was far too wide for Chlotene and me to traverse alone.

Now, sitting with the bible of mental illnesses and disorders open in front of me, I thought, *Could she have a diagnosable mental illness and not "just" be someone with lousy judgment and extreme impulsivity?*

Then I put the thought aside, busy with my own life: an intense schedule of classes, internships, my marriage, taking care of two girls barely out of diapers, and advocating on Tim's behalf to have Phil Jacobs disciplined for sexual abuse.

I had year-long periods where I didn't see Chlotene at all. Then, when I was working toward my master's and my kids were little, she moved to live nearer to us. Nearer as in next door. Or down the block. Or behind our house. She moved a lot.

I had daycare for the kids when I was in school and Tim was at work, and we didn't ask anyone to watch the kids much otherwise. Tim and I didn't do "date nights" or take weekend trips together. But a handful of times, I let Chlotene watch my girls when they were babies.

The tasks involved with watching children required a level of common sense and judgment that she couldn't reach. I realized this when I picked up the girls after she'd watched them for an afternoon. My younger daughter Rachel, who was four, was upset and crying. My mom explained she had spanked Rachel, but for what, she couldn't articulate coherently. When we got home, Rachel told me she didn't want to go back.

I didn't want to wonder or worry, so from then on, we never left the kids with her.

I lived my life. My children grew. I graduated with my master's degree in clinical social work. I completed a postgraduate program in gestalt psychotherapy. I credit Chlotene for my belief in myself during that time. She has always believed I could do anything. I went from call center employee to a master's program graduate.

When I actually started practicing social work, it unnerved me. It was too close. In my first job, I worked with severely mentally ill people at a community mental health center. Then I took a job at a shelter for homeless families. As I worked with homeless single moms, I had no empathy for these women. I was projecting my mom onto them, and I felt defensive for the children upon whom I was projecting myself.

I told myself that I just needed to get out of community mental health and into private practice, where I could work with middle-class folks because I believed they had fixable problems.

7

I KEPT GOING. I kept reaching for safety and security.

I kept trying to take charge. I hounded the Columbus Catholic diocese. When we found out that Father Jacobs had only been transferred to a different church in Canada and hadn't been removed from contact with parishioners or defrocked, we went to the media. Tim was interviewed for the local paper. In 2013, after Jacobs sexually molested a child at a parish in Vancouver, he was finally sentenced to two years probation and registered as a sex offender. He was never charged in Ohio.

As we held the Church to account through the mid-1990s, I worked on finishing my postgraduate studies and finally began work as a gestalt psychotherapist in a group private practice.

I know now that screwed-up people come in every socio-economic description. It wasn't enough to get away from patients living in poverty because ability to pay didn't make a difference. When I was working with dysfunctional people, it all seemed like going back into hell for me.

As I worked in private practice, I truly could not see myself being a therapist for the rest of my life. Not only did it remind me too much of my mom and my own trauma from childhood, but more often than not, therapists don't get to see the results of their work. I wanted results I could claim publicly. I felt impatient with the private, intimate space inherent in a therapy session. I felt smothered, and the work drained me, emotionally and energetically.

I also didn't see a future where I could make enough money to feel safe. I would be tethered to the job, barely making ends meet, but never making a dent in our debts. So, I quit. After three years, I turned my back on the career I thought I had wanted for so long.

I started to read *Rich Dad, Poor Dad* around this time, in about 2000 or so. I picked it up at the library. *Rich Dad* was a juggernaut pop finance book that had been published three years earlier and would soon find its way to the *New York Times* Bestseller List.

At the time and increasingly as the years went, critics questioned the book's advice, to put it mildly. One real estate investor called it "one of the dumbest financial advice books I have ever read."[1] Another personal finance guru, Ramit Sethi, was only a little kinder, writing, "I have grudging respect for this book, but every time someone raves about it, I usually just want to punch them in the face."[2]

I'm glad I didn't run into Sethi back in those days because *Rich Dad* changed the way I thought, and I raved about it to whoever would listen. As Sethi wrote elsewhere about the book, "There are some really great points, like how rich people make money work for them and how everyone else works for money."

That insight—finding ways to make money work for me—landed in the center of my life. I'd always chafed at the hours that Tim and I put in at our jobs and the low wages we got in return. Now I was reading a bestseller that articulated exactly how I'd felt for years.

For another thing, the parable of the dads made *Rich Dad* stick. Robert Kiyosaki, the author, contrasted the way his dad thought about money with his (probably made-up) friend's dad's approach to money. The friend's dad had all the right ideas, the ideas could be boiled down to six easy lessons, and by the time I was done reading, I believed the only thing standing between me and my financial freedom was putting those six lessons to use.

Kiyosaki's shadowy "rich dad" figure connected to an escape from fear and an embrace of freedom. It was a powerful myth I'd bought into over and over in my own life. Dad was the ticket to safety. It was the reason I longed for a dad back in Phoenix. The reason I clung for dear life to Tim's close family and to Tim himself.

I talked to Tim about the book as I read and reread it.

"Uh-huh," he would say. He wasn't excited about it, which was not only completely unsurprising after more than ten years of marriage, but his lack of interest didn't even register in my brain. The pattern was woven into the tapestry of our life. I don't know how I would have reacted if my enthusiasm had sparked something in Tim. He didn't have interests. Or rather, his interests were in keeping his job, going to his job, spending time with our kids and me, and doing what we wanted to do.

It was when I was reading *Rich Dad* that I drove by a vacant storefront near our house. I remember going to Tim with my idea to open a toy store. I presented it to him. My eyes were shining as I told him what I was thinking.

"That storefront on Otterbein Avenue has been vacant for almost a year. And I feel like we could open a store there."

"Yeah?" Tim said.

"I was thinking a toy store would be perfect in there. This town needs a toy store."

"Uh-huh," he said.

"Yeah," I said. I showed him a spreadsheet I'd whipped up earlier in the week, full of grossly inaccurate predictions about startup expenses and revenue projections pulled from my imagination.

"So we need money to do it. We need a small business loan," I said.

"I don't really think it's a good idea for us to go into debt to do this," he said.

"Well, let's see how it goes," I said brightly. "Let's get the numbers, and then we can go from there."

That was the last time Tim pushed back on the idea. With Tim, there was no conflict at all. *I wanna do whatever you wanna do.*

I barreled ahead, sifting through an application for a Small Business Administration loan. They needed a business plan and a budget.

So I created them based on nothing more than what I could find in outdated library books. Needless to say, I was way off. They granted me $27,000. It was a huge loan to me. But it was not even close to being enough to open a retail store. I can't really believe they even granted me the loan, especially now that I run a successful business.

Of course, now I say they granted *me* the loan. But at the time I framed the decision as one Tim and I made together.

I didn't want to admit to myself that I had already made up my mind. I wanted this toy store. I wanted what I wanted, and I was going to make it happen. And I knew that Tim would not stand in my way. But I also knew that I didn't want to be the type of wife who railroaded her husband into decisions. So I needed to feel like he was making the decision too. I pretended to myself that I wanted his input, and I wanted him to help me mull it over.

And that's why both our names appeared on the SBA loan. Both our names appeared on the second mortgage on our house. Both our names appeared on the bankruptcy filing.

Once we were in, Tim was in. He was supportive. He would get behind things even if he wished we hadn't gotten into them in the first place because they were about me and what I wanted.

I didn't reciprocate. I didn't support him in the endeavors he really cared about. Then again, he didn't give me the opportunity. He didn't have any endeavors. He certainly never would have gotten in mind that he wanted to do something like start a business or take a big trip or go back to school, and need my support in those big life pivots. He didn't ask for any of that a single time in all our eighteen years of marriage. He didn't screw shit up and hurt people and grow from his mistakes. He didn't need that kind of partnership at all.

But I did. I carried the weight of driving our life up a hill. I wanted to take us somewhere. What would life look like for us? How would it change? I made those decisions because no one was on the other side with his own ideas. It was a weight. It was a situation I was not helping. I know he was scared to push back because he thought I might get mad. He didn't feel safe.

I know now that if I ask, "What do you think about this?" it's a serious question. I actually want to know what they think.

I listen.

There's discussion.

And, sometimes, I change my mind as a result of what I learn from the discussion.

But with Tim, my asking was a charade.

I had already made up my mind. I pretended to listen. And if he challenged me, then I had a meltdown. Or worse . . . the silent treatment.

So I take responsibility for my part in that. He needed a place that felt safe, and I wasn't safe. Then again . . . who gives a shit how safe it is? It was *his life*. He let me run it.

By 2005 I had been holding myself together for a long time. I was thirty-five. I'd been married for fifteen years. I'd fought the Catholic church, earned two degrees, quit a career in psychotherapy, opened a toy store a month before 9/11. I closed the store in 2003.

My girls, nine and eleven, didn't need me the way small children do, and I found myself seeking again. I was still looking to do work that made a difference. And I got politically active.

So much so that in 2006, I ran for Ohio State Senate.

George W. Bush had been reelected in a landslide in 2004 after starting two devastating wars. I wanted to get involved with people who were trying to *do something* about what they saw was wrong with the world.

I held a meeting at my house for Democrats who were dismayed by the Bush presidency. People were disillusioned like me. At the meeting, we talked about the lack of viable candidates to run against some of the most entrenched Republicans in Ohio state politics. I heard people say that no one was willing to take it on.

"How about you?" a friend suggested after the meeting.

I said no.

Then I said yes, and we started to plan.

At first, I decided to run for State House against an incumbent who'd been there forever. This was one of the seats where the leadership of each party, plus gerrymandering, determined the winner.

I told myself that gerrymandering wasn't the problem, though. The *real* problem, as I saw it, was that the people who had run in the past hadn't talked to enough people. They hadn't been bold enough! Hadn't worked hard enough and tried hard enough. I knew—or thought I knew—I could outwork them.

A few weeks after my decision to run, state Democratic party leadership asked me if I'd consider switching my race from the Ohio House to the Ohio Senate.

I was flattered. I didn't understand at the time that the switch was part of a statewide strategy. If I ran against David Goodman in the third district senate race, they knew that the state Republican party would have to funnel more money than it wanted to our race in order to defeat me. My own party leadership also knew I was guaranteed to lose. But they didn't tell me that.

I was excited. The Democratic party conducted their first poll. I came out ahead: 51 percent to my opponent's 49 percent.

Early buzz! I thought. The party leadership also decided to leak the poll results to the press to alert the opposition. The leak was a commonly used tactic meant to get the Republicans to start spending their money. *Against me.* Spending money on my race would divert their funds from a race in Cleveland where the Democratic candidate had a much better chance of winning.

I didn't know that at the time, though. All I knew was that the poll showed me ahead. It felt good.

Did I sprout into full-blown alcoholism through the course of that exhausting year-long campaign?

No. Maybe.

Before the campaign, we didn't keep alcohol in the house. I may have had wine during the holidays, but when they were over, I went back to my routine and never gave alcohol a second thought. I never used alcohol or other drugs to cope. Never went to bars.

At thirty-five, I had never had a moment in my life when I cut loose or rebelled. I needed to survive as a teenager. I was uptight then, singularly focused on my life-pinnacle goal of graduating high school and lining up a good job so I could move out of Chlotene's grip. Then I married Tim at nineteen, and we spent the next few years scraping by. Then I became a mother. Then Tim revealed the abuse he'd suffered, and I worked for the next decade to save him, to save our semblance of a safe and normal family.

When I was deciding whether to run for office, Chris Redfern, who was about to be elected chair of the Ohio Democratic Party, met with me.

He asked me, "Do you drink?"

At the time I remember thinking, *That is a really strange question.*

"Yeah, at parties and stuff like that," I answered truthfully. "I'm not a big drinker."

"Well, if you do this, get ready to drink more. A lot more."

"What do you mean?" I asked.

"You're just gonna drink more. I've seen it happen," he

replied. Soon after that, he concluded the meeting and gave his blessing to my campaign.

I shrugged it off.

Campaigning brought huge pressures with it, and I was not prepared for a single one of them.

When I held my first press conference at the State House, I said something that didn't sit well with the Democratic Caucus. I got the silent treatment: any in-person meetings I had on the schedule were canceled. It wasn't that the other candidates were mad at me. They just didn't want to associate themselves with someone who went off-script. And "off-script" included directly stating what you were really thinking or what your real intentions were. If you let those thoughts and intentions out of the bag, so much the better for the other side who were just waiting to find out what you actually wanted to accomplish so they could use it against you before you even had the chance to begin.

One of the State House aides gave me a three-ring binder full of lobbyists' contact info. The aide told me to call each person in the book, schedule an in-person meeting with each, and ask for money.

Great! I thought. Made sense to me. Here was a chance for me to show off my work ethic. I started at the top of the list and called every number. As I progressed through the list, I realized most of these people would never meet with me.

Lobbyists had no interest in giving money to anyone but the incumbent. The aide had sent me on a wild goose chase. It was meant to get lobbyists to bring up my name and spur the Republican Caucus to spend money against me. If I was talking to their donors, they might think I was a threat to their own fundraising efforts.

Strategies like that I simply didn't understand. The Democratic Caucus was focused on winning one campaign in Ohio, and it wasn't mine. Still, my campaign had potential. It gained steam, month after month, exactly like a train. Sometimes it went whether I wanted it to or not.

As a candidate, I had to attend so many events: events for my campaign and a whirlwind of events for other candidates. These happy hours and parties were a way to rub shoulders and shake hands. Parades and daytime events happened too, but mostly, these were after-work events held in the evening.

The campaign exposed me to a world that I had never seen. For the first time in my life, I was meeting with powerful people, asking for large donations over lunch, being interviewed at press conferences at the State House, and leading more than one hundred dedicated volunteers. My self-confidence grew out of the sheer repetition of putting myself out there. Besides the near-nightly campaign events, I was also meeting with people at bars, at this thing called "happy hour," which I had never been to before.

I was meeting men who were nothing like my husband and who were interested in me and who were treating me differently from the way Tim did. Shrewd and astute men helped me devise my campaign, advised me on strategy. Took me seriously. Gave me campaign money. I inhabited a world where I was seen as Emily Kreider. Not Tim Kreider's wife. Not my kids' mom. I was Senate candidate Emily Kreider.

From this new perch, I was looking down on the life I was expected to return to if I lost my race, and I knew I couldn't go back there.

I was too busy to attend to that realization, though. Too busy with the campaign and events and happy hour. I never consciously thought about alcohol. But it was becoming an almost daily part of my life.

I never allowed myself to think, *I'm drinking more than I did six months ago.*

More than I did three months ago.

More than I did last month.

That lack of conscious attention made drinking dangerous for me at this time. I wasn't thinking about alcohol, but drinking served as a reliable, anxiety-reducing behavior, month after month, as the campaign unfolded.

One of my first volunteers was my unofficial driver throughout the campaign. He was about sixty, and he was a drinker. He'd even joked once or twice that he was an alcoholic, which didn't mean anything to me. I didn't even understand what alcoholism was. I thought an "alcoholic" was someone who laid in the gutter, literally. I didn't understand alcoholism can develop in anybody who consumes alcohol with enough frequency and in large enough quantities to develop a physical and mental dependency. A need.

I remember one night we were on our way to an event for Chris Redfern, the newly elected Chair of State Democratic Party who had asked me if I drank. On the way there, my volunteer driver and I were chatting about the campaign.

"Why don't we stop off on the way for a drink?" he asked me.

"Great idea," I said.

We'd done it before. Yep! I let him drive me after we'd both been drinking. If I thought about it at all at the time, I told myself that he didn't seem drunk and that he had a higher tolerance to alcohol than me, anyway.

My driver was the first person with whom I'd ever sat at a bar for a drink. I was thirty-six years old. I remember how self-conscious I'd felt the first time we went, which was very early in the campaign. For all of Chlotene's escapades, the fact remains I was raised to sit in church, not at bars. I didn't go to bars in college. Tim and I didn't do "date nights." Even if we did, Tim wasn't in the habit of going to bars or even sitting at the bar in a restaurant.

Whenever we would stop off for a "quick" drink, this volunteer always steered us to the bars of fancy restaurants. At the time, he impressed me as a gentleman. He chose the wine, and he paid the tab (with his company credit card).

Even though I had just one power suit that I wore to everything, I was always well-dressed, my hair and makeup done. I felt put together and sexy, which I hadn't felt in years. I was even wearing earrings!

With all the drinks he paid for, he was probably interested in me. But if he was trying to seduce me, he failed. It wasn't him but the culture of drinking that seduced me. I enjoyed the way I could relax into the back of the barstool and be one person's center of attention while another person poured me a drink in a beautiful glass. I loved the lighting and the sound of conversation around me. I imagined other people in the restaurant knew who I was and watched me play things cool. I enjoyed it, and I craved more of that feeling.

On this particular evening, my volunteer and I stopped off for a drink. Before I knew it, two and a half hours and three glasses of wine had gone by. I felt a little guilty, but I told myself these events were *such a drag*. I told myself I knew I was going to lose my race. Each event became a chore that also seemed totally meaningless.

When we finally pulled into the parking lot for the event that night, Chris Redfern was leaving. I didn't want to get out of the car. I didn't want him to see me. I didn't want to see him. I felt shame, but the feeling was flooded by a sense of relief. *I don't have to go,* I told myself. *I don't have to be there. I don't have to be anywhere.*

As if reading my mind, my driver asked, "Another drink?"

The campaign gave me an ironclad alibi to take home to my family each night as I looked for more opportunities to enjoy the happy hour experience. I was home less and less often, but it made perfect sense as the election neared. Tim and the kids knew why I wasn't there, or I thought they knew. I was doing something important.

My kids struggled. They were in middle school. As the election loomed, my opponent poured more than one million dollars into TV ads alone, and that doesn't count the money he spent on mailers. There were at least six different TV ads that continuously cycled throughout the day and night. I lost count of the full-color glossy fold-out mailers.

My face was everywhere. About eight weeks before election day, his campaign began running attack ads that made it sound like I was the incumbent candidate, and I had missed key votes as a sitting Senator. He was the incumbent, yet he was virtually unknown. He had never needed to campaign for his seat in the Senate. He had never needed to connect with his constituents.

In reality, the ad highlighted my voting record as a private citizen and the primary elections I had missed since I was eighteen years old. The ads were sinister and misleading, which made their incredible effectiveness all the more infuriating. The mailers featured photos of crying children, crying senior citizens, and crying firefighters. If only I'd shown up to "vote"!

Kids were teasing my daughters at school. "Why didn't your mom vote?" they'd screech, and "I saw your mom on TV!"

Once they were in a Taco Bell with some classmates when an attack ad came on. "There's your mom!" one of the kids shouted. They couldn't even go to Taco Bell without my face coming up on TV.

The attack ads were so craven, and I was devastated at how well it worked for my opponent. Together with my volunteers, we knocked on at least five thousand doors over the months, and so many people I met asked me why I had missed so many key votes in the Senate.

"He's attacking my personal voting record," I told each one who asked. "I'm not an elected official. I'm not the sitting senator." I would pause to let that sink in. Then, the light bulb came on. Then, the dismay at being hoodwinked. But it didn't matter. His message played ten, twenty, fifty times a day in some households. I couldn't knock on enough doors.

Volunteers asked me why I didn't run ads in response. "You have to respond! You can't just let him say those things!" they said.

"It takes money to create commercials and run ads on TV," I said, stating the obvious. *It also takes more than the fifty- and hundred-dollar donations that my campaign is built on.*

Winning required the big money donations that only incumbents get in this state. And I couldn't break that awful news to my supporters. I had to keep going.

Every Saturday of the campaign, I met my volunteers in a parking lot with coffee and donuts. I gave them campaign flyers and literature, and we'd all go out. They were really committed.

If you're willing to show up, people will show up, I learned. You just have to ask them. Not everyone will show up if you ask, of course. But some people are just looking for someone to take the lead. That experience had an effect on what I think is possible—in my life, in the world.

That experience taught me that "taking the lead" in life is not forcefully taking charge and trying to control everything, but actually just showing up and asking for help.

But along with that lesson came so much bitterness. In the end, I lost, just as everyone had predicted. I earned 45.9 percent of the vote to my opponent's 54.1 percent. The state Democratic Party's strategy to force the Republicans to divert money from more competitive races to my race had certainly worked. His campaign had had to spend a total of $1.3 million to claw back those five percentage points from that first poll, taken almost a year earlier.

I always joke, "I came in second!" But the loss shredded me. I'd told myself for weeks before the election I was sure to lose. I'd prepared in every way. But I was still crushed.

8

TIM NEVER SAID anything about my new pattern of drinking during the course of my State Senate campaign. Not when I would come home later than I had promised smelling like a bar. Not when I started the daily habit of relaxing on the couch at home with two, then three beers after an evening of walking door-to-door. The routine of reading or playing games with my daughters in the evenings was replaced with a drink or three instead.

What should he have said?

Now, I was done with that campaign. It was over. I decided that I was going to divorce my husband. I can't pinpoint the moment I knew I was going to end our marriage. But by the end of the campaign, I knew Tim couldn't give me the life that I had just spent the past year sampling. And I wanted it. I was sure of that. I didn't talk about my decision with anyone, least of all Tim, but I knew it.

I lost in November 2006, and by December, I'd gotten the highest-paying job I'd ever had to sell textbooks for Pearson. I started on the first weekday after New Year's, January 2007.

Within a few days, I was headed to the national sales meeting in Phoenix. The sales team all drank copiously and gregariously. When I got back from Phoenix, I continued to go out with them after work, but I couldn't very easily sell this socializing to my husband and kids as part of my job, the way I could during the campaign as mom's "important work."

I told Tim I was moving out but that it was a trial separation. I just needed some time and space, I said. But when I got my own apartment in March 2007, I knew I wouldn't be back.

When I left Tim after seventeen years of marriage, my model for relationships was my mother's model. When she didn't know what else to do, she bailed out. She cut off relationships. She kicked people out of her home. She quit jobs. She abandoned anything that could keep her from escaping.

That's how I approached the divorce. Facing the shame I felt about my own behavior in our marriage, setting boundaries, or being honest didn't even occur to me as real options. Maybe I knew these things on an intellectual level. I had certainly absorbed something about marriage and honesty in my professional training as a therapist. But my behavior pattern with Tim was set. I wasn't emotionally mature enough to endure the shame or set the boundaries.

My relationship with Tim made me feel stuck, and I had grown tired of the mundanity of our life for a long time before I started my Senate run. I loved my kids, but I had never been satisfied by the day-to-day labor of caretaking, especially when they were small. Setting it all to one side for a few months felt like a relief to me. Working toward the goal of winning the race—a goal that had nothing to do with my family—gave me an escape. When it was over, I couldn't go back.

Tim was passive in our relationship, but he also had qualities that I didn't appreciate until after our divorce was final and I was engaged to another man in 2008. Tim was kind. He was a good dad to our kids. He was supportive. But he didn't seem to want us to go anywhere else as life partners. And I didn't know how to tell him I found our stasis stifling or what he would have said if I had. So I didn't tell him anything at all.

As for the kids, they were teenagers, wrapped up in their friends and peer relationships. I wanted to give them space to individuate, the space I never had, growing up with Chlotene.

I rationalized that they were fine without me, anyway. Throughout the campaign, when I wasn't home evening after evening, I noticed that their world didn't fall apart. Tim and the girls functioned great without me, I told myself. Tim picked up the slack: everyone got to school and got home and ate and got to bed. They didn't need me, I said to myself.

But that was all bullshit. I was giving myself excuses that enabled me to be on my own more so I could drink as much as I wanted without fear of discovery or judgment. Without a husband and kids who all knew what I had been like before I started to drink, it was easier for me to deny how obsessed I'd become with drinking. I wanted to hide from them, but I couldn't even admit that to myself.

The truth: *I* was the one who needed space, even though I told myself my daughters did. At the time, the compulsion to drink went hand in hand with my compulsion for my own space. I couldn't deny my need anymore. I wanted to build a new life. I wanted them in my life, but I also wanted to date. I wanted to find another man who was nothing like Tim. I wanted things that I had missed out on by getting married at nineteen. I wanted to go out into this world and party.

I know it was all the more painful for both my kids because my behavior changed all throughout their high school years. I was becoming a mom they didn't recognize and didn't respect. They were angry with me, and I can't blame them.

They couldn't understand my decision to leave their dad. Even before then, when I opened the store and when I ran my campaign. I based so many decisions on what I wanted to do, not on trying to find a fulfilling combination of what I wanted to do and what would have been best for them. They fought me, then they avoided me, and I rationalized too much of it away as "normal teenage individuating."

I had met Tim when I was a teenager myself. He helped me make my escape from a life with Chlotene permanent. A relationship with Tim brought with it a whole family and a Catholic community. Things for me to belong to. And I took that chance with him. But twenty years later, with two teen girls, a bachelor's, a master's, a failed business, and a State Senate run all behind me . . . I wanted to party. So I did.

We worked out a joint custody arrangement where I had my kids every other week. I left almost my entire life behind me. The house, the extended family, my identity as a mom in a family . . . and it felt like an escape. My drinking escalated during the weeks without my kids. I believed my drinking was under control because I didn't get drunk when my kids were around. But, before long, I just timed my level of intoxication with the time I could expect them to go to bed. Then, I'd be up for a few more hours drinking before I passed out. I picked up a six-pack or a bottle of wine every night.

I was sowing wild oats, meeting men out for drinks and sometimes sleeping with them, having fun. After the separation, I was unreliable and impulsive. I was selfish. Of course, I could have engaged in all those behaviors and still not have been an alcoholic.

But I was becoming preoccupied with opportunities to drink. A drink to relax. A drink while cooking. A drink during dinner. A drink with a guy. Drinks with coworkers. Drinking had become the way to do this new life. Normal. Not a problem.

And I know it hurt my kids, although they never confronted me about my drinking or my behavior. I married my second husband, Pete, in August 2008, a year and a half after I'd moved out and six months after my divorce from their father was final. We organized our honeymoon as a family vacation, with Pete's kids and my kids coming with us.

It was on this trip that my back began to hurt. Big time. Within a month of getting married, I had emergency back surgery, which was followed by another major surgery three months later.

I was managing my pain with opioids and fentanyl patches and alcohol. In the fall of 2008, between my first and second back surgeries, my girls took care of me. They put my shoes on for me. They did our grocery shopping. (Except for alcohol. Pete made sure we always had wine in the fridge.)

I was an invalid, even after the second surgery in 2009, which took months of recovery. I couldn't attend any of their school functions. My older daughter, Barbara, had learned how to drive, and she would drive her sister, Rachel, to work or to her piano lessons. Rachel got her license as soon as she was eligible. I never had a problem giving them the keys to my car because it meant I didn't have to go anywhere.

My back eventually got better, but my drinking continued to progress. I was waking up in the morning, looking at the clock, and saying to myself, "I hardly got anything done yesterday. I'll skip drinking today." Then I would work furiously throughout the day until I ran out of gas. Exhausted by 5:00 p.m., I rewarded all of my hard work that day with just one glass of wine. Then two. And so on.

It took years for that 5:00 p.m. marker to move to 4:00 p.m., and then 3:00, and eventually 11:30 in the morning. Eventually, the timing of my start no longer mattered. Drinking had become the center of my attention no matter what time it was.

The central position of alcohol in my life was subtle. When I opened my eyes each morning, I asked myself, "What do I need to get done today?" The remainder of that question was implied.

What do I need to get done today before I can have my first drink?

After all, I wanted to be productive. But the bar for "getting stuff done" kept getting lower. I accomplished less and less until afternoons consisted mostly of pacing in front of the living room window with a glass of wine or beer.

Everything in my life became about drinking, including dealing with the consequences of drinking. I'd forget what I had said, but my husband or my kids would still be angry with me for having said it. I'd forget to show up to an appointment or miss a deadline.

I'd rotate the stores where I bought my alcohol, alternating between supermarkets and smaller grocery stores and liquor stores, because I didn't want any of the cashiers to raise an eyebrow. If it was Thursday or Friday, I might tell the cashier, "We're having a party this weekend," even though she hadn't asked.

If we were planning on going out for dinner, I made sure to steer us clear of Cracker Barrel. Or Bob Evans. Or fast-food restaurants. I would say I didn't like the food at those places, but it wasn't about the food. Going to a restaurant that didn't serve alcohol would interfere with the opportunity to drink.

The closest either of my daughters came to confronting me was when Barbara uninvited me from her high school graduation party in 2011, years after I had become dependent on alcohol. At the time I was completely shocked.

"What do you *mean*?" I whined to her on the phone when she told me not to come. "I'm your mother! I'll just come anyway."

"Please don't do that," she said.

When I pressed her for an explanation, she told me Tim's siblings and the extended Kreider family weren't "over" our divorce. She said she didn't want to be caught in the middle.

I was so angry with Tim. So good at playing the martyr, I thought. But when I called him to demand an explanation, he told me he had no problem with me coming to the party. "It's her," he said, leaving the entire thing at Barbara's feet.

I knew he was telling me the truth. She had made the decision on her own. I had lost her. I recognized that feeling of "being done with my mom," and I felt so sad about it. But I didn't know what to do. When I looked back at her high school years, I could only see the problems I had created. I didn't see my alcoholism as the source of those problems.

I believed I was done parenting. They had so many activities! So many friends! But I was abandoning them, leaving them to sort through their feelings about a separation and divorce they couldn't have seen coming.

After the phone call with Tim, I left it there. I attended her graduation, didn't attend the party, and we never discussed it again.

I decided to leave Tim in 2007, and that was the right decision, but I handled it all wrong. My girls were fifteen and thirteen, and I believed I was done being a mom. I betrayed them.

From 2008 to 2011, I remarried twice. Twice in three years. My daughters felt like they didn't know me. Before I started drinking, I had been married to their dad for seventeen years.

Getting married was my version of a "geographic cure." I wasn't in a position to move across the country to escape my problems—or I would have. Instead, I switched husbands.

Once I left Tim, every time my life felt out of control, I started dating a new man. The only problem with the geographic cure—and my serial monogamy version of it—is that it's not a cure at all. Alcoholics take themselves with them when they move. So did I. I brought myself with me into each relationship. Into each of my next two marriages.

I shook up my life again to get rid of what I had created, just like Chlotene had every time she moved apartments. Every time she quit. But just as it had for her, the Etch A Sketch filled up again with a mess of lines that led nowhere and depicted nothing.

I needed to drink, but I didn't *think* I needed to drink. I just drank with the quantity and frequency creeping up slowly enough that my dependency on alcohol could continue to feel normal. It had become a reflex.

Leave. Bail out. Abandon. Cut off relationships. Don't let anyone or anything stop you from going. Chlotene's disease was schizophrenia. Mine was alcoholism. My brain chose alcohol over doing the difficult work of facing the shame I felt about leaving. There was no one left in my life that would confront me with the truth about my drinking.

By 2011 I was married to my third husband, Mark. My older daughter, Barbara, was in college, and my younger daughter, Rachel, was in her senior year of high school.

That year, I voluntarily gave up my custody rights, and Rachel never lived with us. We didn't even have a discussion about whether she would live with us half time until she called me, one week after my third spinal surgery in June 2011. She was wondering if she should start staying over every other week. "So am I just living with Dad now?" she asked.

I told her it "just made sense" that she would stay with her dad—as if I was just doing what was best for her. After all, my second ex-husband, Pete, was stalking me, and I was living with Mark on the other side of town from her dad's house. Better to live with Dad full-time.

That's how far I was willing to go. I gave that up. I gave her up in her last year of childhood.

At the time, I told myself we were all on the same page. She was relieved not to have to play house with me and yet another husband she didn't know. Mark didn't want her to live with us. Neither did Tim. I told myself I didn't want to *make her* live with us. My marriage to Mark was chaotic, and his home was so cluttered and dirty that most people would have considered it unlivable. I wouldn't admit it at the time, but I felt shame. I didn't want her to have to witness my home life.

But ultimately, I chose to be with a man who would look

the other way when I drank, instead of my daughter, who wouldn't have put up with my drunkenness. She would have said something about my drinking, and we would have fought. I didn't want the fight. I was too fragile to face even the possibility of a moment of that, too committed to denial and alcohol.

So I gave up joint custody. Then I minimized and justified my decision so that I could keep drinking.

I remember, somewhere around this time, drunk-dialing my other daughter Barbara and carrying on about something or other. After a few minutes, she cut me off.

"Have you been drinking?" she asked.

"No!" I responded, clutching my imaginary pearls. "Why would you say that?"

PART III

"You're gonna be mad at me."
"Well, tell me what happened, and we'll see. What did you do?"

9

For all of 2014, I had not had a drink. But I wasn't in recovery. I wasn't "working" any program. I didn't want to change the way I approached my life. I *certainly* didn't call myself an alcoholic.

I didn't want to take on an identity that conjured up an image in my mind of a dependent and unreliable woman with poor judgment. "Alcoholic" was someone who was out of control. Someone living on the edge of society. Sleeping on the floor of someone else's apartment. Weak-minded.

I'd worked my entire life to get away from being an out-of-control person who lived on the edge. I repeated, "I will never be like my mom" to myself so often throughout my adult life that it was practically a mantra.

But even after months of abstaining from alcohol, I was still living on the edge—maybe not on the edge of society, but on the edge of something.

Of course, before my year of "cold turkey" abstention, I had "decided" to give up drinking dozens of times. Usually I decided when I was puking my guts out. Late at night, I would drink until I was sick. Then I'd pass out for a while and wake up and run to the toilet. As I was retching, I felt so physically awful I told myself I knew that time would be the last time.

No more, I would think.

But by morning, the thought of a drink came to mind, and I felt no need to resist.

My next drink was always on my mind.

What do I need to get done today?

So, when I did stop drinking in 2014, it was because I had been introduced to Alcoholics Anonymous. After attending only a few AA meetings, I could no longer deny that alcohol was a problem for me. I couldn't stay sober for more than a few weeks at first. I didn't want to accept this new identity of alcoholic. So I hung out around the edges. As the months passed, it didn't get easier *not* to drink. I was getting tired, the fatigue steadily eroding my motivation.

I was hanging on by my fingertips to the ledge of my alcohol-free streak. My physical dependency on alcohol had left me within just a few days, but the mental obsession pried at my grip. I avoided alcohol, but I didn't have a way to move on from alcohol.

I had stopped drinking because I hated the way my life looked and felt when I drank. But here I was drink-free, and drinking was still at the center of my life, which I hadn't expected.

Now that I wasn't drunk every day, I could see that I really shouldn't drink. But it wasn't clear to me that I shouldn't drink forever. I imagined that, after a while, circumstances around me would change without me having to do anything else. My relationship would "get better" on its own. Or maybe I'd become one of those people who didn't need a romantic relationship. I would be financially independent.

Sure, I noticed that because I wasn't drinking, I didn't have to deal with being hungover all the time. I noticed that Mark and I didn't fight as much. I didn't have to deal with my shame over what I'd said or done when I was drunk. I didn't have to remember with a pang how insulting I'd been the night before, the hurtful, idiotic things I'd said.

But those changes weren't going to be enough to keep me away from drinking forever. If anything, I could use the improvements I'd made as evidence that I wasn't really an alcoholic. To tell myself that I would drink differently once I had everything in my life squared away. I was already bargaining with myself.

Every now and then, I'd show up to a recovery meeting, usually after a fight with Mark. I'd sit in those meetings and silently catalog all the ways I didn't fit in with the other people there. Even though a meeting would help me get through that day, I still wanted to believe I wasn't one of *them*.

Other times, I plowed some of my obsessive thinking into work and building my business. I'd started my website development business in 2012, and my prices were too low, so I was buried in work but barely making a profit. The nonstop work did have the benefit of distracting me, and I worked until it was time to go to bed so that I wouldn't drink. I'd pass out from exhaustion instead of alcohol.

The constant work wasn't enough to calm my tumultuous third marriage, though. Tumultuous . . . as in me breaking shit. Throwing stuff. Yelling. Slamming doors—not just once but over and over again until pictures fell off the adjoining wall. Once I had quit drinking, my reason for marrying Mark in the first place became obvious. I no longer needed someone to pay for or tolerate my drinking. My dependency on him slowly evaporated.

I'd left Mark briefly, about a year after we were married. I signed a six-month lease on an apartment and moved into it one day without warning him. He came to get me, and we moved back in together that same month. But we were constantly fighting and never happy.

Even the literal day I married him in February 2011, I could hear a clear voice in my head saying, "I don't want to do this. And now it's too late." But I did it. I married him. It was just one more bad decision.

"When I marry him, things will be different," my brain said. "Marrying him will be a fresh start," it said, disregarding the fact that Mark never questioned my drinking and had no problem with the way I drank. What could possibly change?

In fact, back then, as I was careening through full-blown alcohol dependency, one of the bright spots about our relationship was that Mark never suggested to me that I had a drinking problem. Not once. Which is really very weird because I was usually drunk when he got home from work. I was in total denial about my drinking problem, so his denial or inability to see my drinking fit right in with what I wanted: someone who would never question my drinking habits or kick up any of my buried shame.

When we would fight, he would bring up past things I'd done or said. Or past conversations we'd had together. Things that I didn't remember because I'd been drunk.

But drinking *couldn't* be the reason for my memory lapses,

I thought. It couldn't be that I was an alcoholic. Instead, I decided I must have early-onset Alzheimer's at the age of forty-two.

I found an online diagnostic test that tells you whether you might have Alzheimer's. (I know, super reliable.) But at the time I was eager to take it. I passed. No Alzheimer's.

"That can't be right," I said. "There's something wrong with the test."

I had Mark take the test. He passed too. I took it again. I passed again.

Why don't I remember the things Mark says I've said? I asked myself.

That's how badly I didn't want to be an "alcoholic." I didn't want alcohol-fueled blackouts to be the reason for my not remembering. Mark never blamed my drinking for my "forgetfulness" either. Instead, he thought I was a liar. I could live with that label, though, because at least we were joined together in the denial of my alcoholism.

He also didn't say anything when I *stopped* drinking in 2014. At that point, I had no friends at all, and no support, which was a bed I'd made for myself over many years. I hadn't had big blowups with people. I just didn't know how to be a friend to anyone. I didn't show up when friends needed me, I didn't listen, and I could only function in relationships where the other person was trying to fix me or save me because I had nothing to bring to the table. That got old really fast for people. My daughters were keeping their distance. Life had become small.

In the years before I stopped drinking, I would bring my laptop and sit at a table in the bar area of a local sports bar so that I felt less like a drunk. I'd order food, too, so that I could make my day-drinking seem somehow more normal. The bartender knew my name and had my beer already poured for me when she came to my table at one in the afternoon. I over-tipped. I don't know why. She always seemed like the happiest person to see me that day.

Yet, when I showed up to an AA meeting, those alcoholics were always happy to see me. They acted like they missed me. As 2014 wore on, I knew I shouldn't drink, but I still wasn't sure if AA was "right for me."

Part of my mental obsession with drinking led me to think compulsively about whether I might be an alcoholic and then to think of all the reasons why I definitely wasn't one.

I kept attending meetings and eventually strung together several weeks of sobriety, which then turned into months without a drink. But I was hanging on by a thread. My willingness to identify as an alcoholic and commit to a program of recovery was tenuous. My grip on the ledge of abstinence was just about to slip completely. I would have started drinking again at some point that year or the next because I was still in denial. I still believed I could control alcohol in my life.

My third marriage wasn't going any better than the rest of my life, either. I was still stuck, and I was ready to say, "Fuck it!"

———

Mark had his own problems, and denying those took up the bulk of his energy. The times that I'd been to his house before we were married, I could see his problems. They lay in literal piles all over the house. I told myself that Mark was "just messy."

I'd look at the stacks and stacks of paper. It was hard not to look at them since there was no place to sit unless you first moved a stack of mail and papers and magazines. If there was a magazine, he subscribed to it. They were everywhere.

Well, he doesn't collect things, I told myself. *He just has a lot of stuff. But it's not obsessive.*

He certainly did have a lot of stuff. On every flat surface, he had stuff. Table, counters, the stovetop. Besides papers, he had dozens and dozens of broken appliances and electronics. He had a gas dryer next to the electric dryer that actually functioned in the house where we lived.

The trash cans were always overflowing, pouring garbage from the top like a bottle of shook-up champagne so that each one had a wreath of trash around the base.

And that odor? *What odor?*

When I walked into his house, I didn't let the odor penetrate the sentence level of my brain.

At the time I didn't understand anything about hoarding. But when I walked into his house after just a few dates and I saw *that garbage* everywhere, on every surface, that should have been the end. But it wasn't. I needed a partner, and I needed someone who wouldn't question my drinking. Mark filled the bill.

Even if I had understood hoarding, I don't think I would have been able to admit to myself at the time that he was a hoarder.

I remember the first time my daughters came over.

Rachel paused in the doorway, and her eyes grew big. "What's that smell?" she whispered.

I bit my lower lip and said nothing.

After we got married, we had a fight, and I told him I would not move into his house until it was clean. Well, OK, if not clean, then clean-*er*. He did nothing, so I lived in another house for a while after we were married. I was undergoing my third surgery in three years. The cleaning-out process was so emotional for Mark. He couldn't let go of a single item.

So I did it for him. I cleaned up his messes, sometimes literally following behind him with a broom and a dustpan, cleaning up as soon as he would leave a room. I called a junk collection truck when he was out of the house. They came and removed several truckloads from the basement. As they drove away for the last time, I was dismayed to see they'd barely made a dent. In fact, it was so insignificant that Mark didn't even notice!

I was a little elf with a dustpan who rearranged furniture and opened mail so that we didn't miss important bills. Just like I'd been as a child around Chlotene.

The life I'd chosen with Mark was almost too "on the nose." Not only did I spend hours and hours of my time each day, each week, trying to clean up a mess that I didn't make and couldn't fix (ironic), I was also constantly fighting with him, trying to force him to see what was in front of his face but what he would never see.

"This is crazy," I'd say as he burst into tears or angrily accused me of trying to steal something away from him. Every *thing* was important, and I was the enemy for wanting to get rid of anything.

"Take responsibility for this mess!" I kept saying.

But he refused to admit it *was* a mess. He didn't willfully refuse; he was just blind to his hoarding being a problem. So even when he cleaned around the edges or consented to me decorating a bit or hanging pictures on the walls, he couldn't really change the way he lived. And that meant I couldn't either.

About a year into our marriage, I heard a radio segment about hoarding. The expert talked about the fact that hoarding was not a personality problem or a bad habit. It was a mental illness. No amount of persuading or confrontation would change that. They even talked about the fact that researchers had found real *visible* differences in the brain scans of hoarders versus non-hoarders.

The click inside my brain was almost audible.

"Mark has a disability," I said to myself. "My job isn't to force him to take responsibility, because he can't." It was the first time I ever considered letting go of the job of trying to get him to be different. But I didn't let go of the hope that we could stay married. I didn't want to be divorced for a third time.

I didn't see it at the time, but this realization made a huge dent in the way I thought about Chlotene's behavior and, eventually, in the way I thought about my own. I was so busy in my adult life with getting other people to behave themselves. To act right.

I made it my mission to bring Tim's abuser to some kind of justice. I got my master's in social work because I wanted "to help people." Here I was now, literally chasing my husband around with a broom and dustpan.

When I listened to that radio story, it was the first time I thought to myself, *What if I just stopped?*

And that realization became key to all the ways in which my life would change a few months later.

Meanwhile, Mark was suspicious of me. I often had no income during our marriage, and he accused me of using him or trying to steal his money. I kept trying to talk Mark out of it.

That's where we were in October 2014.

10

THROUGHOUT 2014 I focused on building my new business and not drinking, while Chlotene had been more and more severely losing touch with reality.

I had been distracted since 2008. There was my alcohol dependence, my two divorces and three marriages, and my three back surgeries. And now I was burying myself in the work of building my own website development business.

Since I had stopped drinking, I could maintain a great relationship with my computer. It did what I told it to do—usually. My work gave me instant results: make an edit, click refresh, and *voila*! Results.

My work had become an escape—one that replaced alcohol.

I had even joined a local networking group that met every week. Interaction with real people! I began to feel capable. I still wasn't sure if I could support myself financially, but there was a light at the end of the tunnel.

Functional relationships with the people closest to me were another story. Nothing had changed about my relationship with Mark except that I could now remember what I said in all our conversations. After several months without alcohol, my reasons for marrying Mark in the first place were laid bare and beginning to evaporate.

I rarely saw my daughters.

But I still maintained enough of a connection with Chlotene, and I had enough perspective, based on all I knew about her, to notice that she'd been calling me several times a week to tell me about what "they" were doing next door.

The neighbors were kidnapping and raping women. They were prostituting them. My daughters were there. She was worried. Were they a part of "it"?

Once she took a cab to my house after I married Mark. She'd tried to call me, and I hadn't answered. Mark opened the door, and she said accusingly, "Where's my daughter? Is she OK? Let me see her!"

Once I came to the door, I fell into my familiar role of reassurance. "Hey, Mom," I said. "What're you doing here?"

"You didn't answer your phone," she said. "Where were you?"

The visit jarred Mark. He didn't like opening the door to my distraught mother, her finger in his face. I told him he was exaggerating. What was the big deal? I said. She wanted to check on me, and when she saw that I was OK, she went away.

But inside, I knew exactly what the big deal was. I knew the reason why my mother had never lived with me as an adult and why I would never allow her to. The reason she never babysat my children once they were old enough to tell me through tears that she'd spanked one of them. Her paranoia contained as much menace as it had when I was young. Could I be sure she wouldn't attack Mark one day, wrapped up in some warped paranoid fantasy about what he was trying to do to me? She wasn't safe.

The calls came more often, and more often in the middle of the night.

When I picked up, she might say, "I could hear you talking in Hildy's apartment." Hildy was a neighbor who lived in her building two floors below.

It was pointless to ask Chlotene how she could possibly think she could hear me from the receiving end of a phone of a neighbor who lived two floors down.

So I just said, "Are you sure it was me?"

She called my daughters too. They were college-age by this time and had phones of their own. They stopped answering.

She complained that her neighbor's TV volume was so loud, and she was sure the neighbor was doing it on purpose to "conceal her activities."

I rolled my eyes and moved on to other topics of conversation, but soon I couldn't move to any topic without her referring back to one of her delusions.

She sent daily emails to groups of people—some of her own children, my two daughters, other relatives. But she also included strangers on the list I didn't know and would never meet. The emails were mostly astrological updates, but they made less and less sense, even within the parameters of their own strange logic.

August 16, 2014:
> . . . Also, I have a suspicion that my neighbors are calling people and places I used to know and are asking them for money for utilities, doctor bills, etc. Please don't let anybody we know be fooled by this scam. It may have been going on for a long time. Geeeez! I could spend all day saying why I want to get away from here, or get rid of my neighbor that uses my name all of the time.

Once, around this time, I was standing with her in the parking lot of her apartment building, leaning against my car. Before my brain could stop the words from tumbling out, I asked her, "Mom, do you think any of this stuff you're saying about your neighbor might be going on in your head?"

Her eyes glittered, and I saw a shadow of the tsunami that regularly crashed over me when I was a kid. The way her eyes looked when she'd pounced on Joan back in Arizona and screamed at her to get out. The way her eyes looked when she slapped the taste out of my mouth after I told a neighbor we were unloading free groceries from the local food pantry.

"No. ABSOLUTELY NOT," she fumed.

Why would I say that? How dare I even hint at such a thing? How dare anyone question her?

I backpedaled, recoiling from her anger. "Well, I'm just trying to consider all the options," I said. "I don't know what's going on."

She didn't answer. For a while after that day, she wouldn't speak to me at all.

But the emails kept coming. She peppered in so many charming anecdotes and astrological updates, always keeping them halfway to eccentric.

Hello, this is Chlo

Moon slipped from Saggitarius into Capricorn last nite [sic] between 1:08a and 8:31a this morning.

Capricorn is a sign for organization, practicality and being business like. Caution and pessimism in the air. Do not act too businesslike for the sake of others.

At the Embassy: We are having a special meeting here, about safety and security on Wednesday.

It will be led by the Property Managers. They will answer safety and security questions. Every resident is requested to be there. I have my list of questions and suggestions ready. After all, we are in Capricorn.

"The Embassy" was her joke name for her apartment building. Not a delusion, of course! Just the cute eccentricity of a little old lady.

A few months later, she was moving out of "The Embassy"—another move—and I had helped her find a new senior apartment complex. She'd signed the lease in late October 2014. Then she called me about 9:00 a.m. one day in early November.

"Hello?"

"Emily. Hi. Well . . . I did something bad."

"What?"

"I did something bad. I'm in trouble."

"Why?"

"You're gonna be mad at me."

"What did you do?"

I sat down on the living room couch.

"Just tell me what happened," I said, trying to sound casual.

"Well, my neighbor has a Halloween decoration on her door . . ." she said.

Oh, boy, I thought. *Did she tear down this poor woman's Halloween decoration?*

". . . so I lit a match to it. I'm just so tired of what she's doing! She's playing the TV loud on purpose so that people can't hear what's going on over there. I can still—"

I interrupted her. "A match? Did it catch fire?"

"Well, it made a lot of smoke. I tried to put it out right away."

"Did the smoke alarm go off?" I asked.

"Yeah, and the doors closed," she said, referring to the emergency fire doors, which automatically triggered shut in case of fire on either end of the long hallway.

"When they closed, it scared me, so I ran to the kitchen and got a glass of water and threw it on the door, and I ran back to the kitchen and got another glass of water, and I threw it! But she opened the door, and I threw it in her face," Chlotene said, a giggle bubbling up with the last three words. "But then the fire department came. And there were so many! And . . . I mean, *I* put the fire out before they even got there. It was just a lot of smoke."

I sat down on the couch and started rubbing my forehead with my free hand.

"The fire department? What did they say to you?" I asked.

"Well, they didn't really say anything. But then the police came."

"Oh no," I whispered. "Mom . . . were they . . . what did they ask you?"

"They came inside my apartment. And I was crying. They told me it was gonna be OK. I don't wanna go to jail!"

"Is that what you told them, Mom?"

"Well, yeah! I don't want to go to jail!"

"Wait, did they arrest you?" I asked.

"Well, they were looking at the tarot deck on my table.

They were looking through the deck, and they asked me about the fire card. Of course, that's not even what that means. That's what I told them!"

"Oh no," I groaned. "This is a big deal. This is a really big deal, Mom. What else? Tell me exactly what you told them."

"I told them everything! I didn't know it would make so much smoke! The fire was out before the fire department got there."

What did they tell you to do next?"

"The detective left his card here," she told me. "He wants you to bring me into the station."

"OK," I said. "Give me the number."

I took her to the police station the next day. They took her mugshot, fingerprinted her, and we left. Her apartment complex happened to be across the street from the station. As we were walking home, I said, "I'm going to make an appointment with a psychiatrist, and we're gonna do whatever the psychiatrist tells us to do. I really need you to come to that appointment."

It felt urgent. It felt like I needed to help Chlotene demonstrate she was getting some kind of treatment, even though I wasn't expecting a SWAT team to show up or any of the rest of what was coming.

Chlotene worried about prison. A lot. She brought it up several times. By this time, I'd known for years that she'd actually been to prison and given birth in prison in 1966. She never said it, but it was clear that although she still believed her delusions and even believed she had a good reason for setting the fire, she also remembered prison and knew she didn't want to go back.

Throughout this time, I'd say over and over, "You're not going to jail, Mom." I heard in my empty reassurance the echo of the voice of child-Emily, always prepared to reassure Chlotene about anything and everything.

"We can still get to Ohio, Mom. It's gonna be OK."

"If my dad comes by, that doesn't mean I'll move in with him or something. Come on, mom! Why would I leave you?"

And now, "You're not going to jail! We just have to do all the right things."

Just like it had throughout my life, my reassurance calmed her down, at least temporarily. But she worried anyway. That worry was at least partially the reason she agreed to see a psychiatrist. She was even grateful that I might save her from a fate she could see unspooling before her.

So I got to work on getting an appointment for her. A few days later, Dr. Baker welcomed us into her office. She looked very young to me, thirty at most. In my head I was calculating how long she could have possibly been a doctor.

How long do medical school, residency, and a potential post-residency fellowship program take? Eight years? Ten?

"What's brought you in today?" she said, interrupting my thoughts.

I had prepared what I wanted to say, and I launched in. "I want to say some things to my mom as a part of communicating to you."

Before the appointment, I had decided to open with some positive, appreciative thoughts for my mom. I imagined that during this visit, the doctor would give Chlotene a formal diagnosis and prescribe medication—two things I'd never seen Chlotene face. I also knew that I wanted Chlotene to be as willing as possible to take the doctor's advice, and I hoped that what I was about to say would make her more compliant. The appointment felt important. Consequential.

"Mom," I said, "I want you to know that we've had a really hard time. But there are some really good things about me that I get from you. So one of the things I love about myself is that I'm hilarious."

She giggled.

"It's true. You are really funny, Mom. You make people laugh, and I'm the same way." I continued, "I also get my intelligence from you. You are really smart."

"Well, sometimes I don't feel like I am," Chlotene said.

"Well, you are," I said. "And I get that from you. The third thing I get from you is this belief in myself that I can do anything. You have always believed in me. That means a lot to me. I'm able to do the important things I do because you've believed in me."

"Yes, Emily," she said, looking at me. "You can do anything you want."

I looked her directly in the eyes before continuing. I'd said how much I appreciated Chlotene because I needed a way to tell myself that I wasn't a bad daughter for what I was about to say next. In that moment I felt guilty, and I did feel like I might be a bad daughter for deciding not to sign off on her refusal to seek help.

The moment passed.

"So," I said, "I want the doctor to understand your history." I told the doctor the details about the fire. Then I said, "Is that what happened, Mom?"

"Yes, it is," Chlotene replied.

"It's because my mom believes certain things," I said.

The doctor turned to focus on me. I didn't know where Chlotene was looking; I avoided her gaze. Teetering between guilt and resolve, I continued. "She believes that her neighbor is running a prostitution ring . . . and this is a senior housing complex, OK? She thinks people are being held hostage. She thinks she can hear conversations downstairs that are clearly out of earshot. She thinks she can hear both sides of a phone conversation on the first floor on the other side of the building, when she lives on the third floor."

I continued to keep my eyes forward, careful not to look at Chlotene for fear her reaction would silence me before I was finished. I was, for once, speaking the whole truth about my mother's illness to someone who didn't seem like she was going to crumple any of it into a tight crinkly ball and toss it away.

"How long has this been going on?" asked Dr. Baker.

"Well, that's really happening. I have really good hearing," said Chlotene, before I could answer.

I kept my gaze fixed on Dr. Baker as I said, "Mom, you have been hearing voices your whole life. And it's always the neighbors! Don't you think that's strange that you always have a problem with neighbors?"

"Yeah," she replied credulously, "I don't know what it is about me!"

"Mom," I said, finally turning to her. "Tell her about the time you saw Osama bin Laden."

My mom launched into the story. The nursing home. Tall man syndrome. The turban touching the ceiling.

Dr. Baker took it all in stride. She asked a few more questions. "Have you ever taken psychiatric medication? Have you ever been hospitalized?"

As the thirty-minute visit was ending, Dr. Baker said, "I'm going to recommend immediate hospitalization so that Ms. Tubbs can get stabilized. She's set a fire, and it's clear she is a danger to others."

I was shocked. *Wow,* I thought. *Hospitalization. This really is serious!*

That moment brought me validation, which brought me

relief. Chlotene had an illness, which meant she had options for treatment. A path to follow.

All these years, without a professional diagnosis, I found I couldn't *really* say, "My mom has schizophrenia."

I no longer felt pressure to minimize Chlotene's condition or her actions. Now I had to find out whether she would continue to deny help.

"Are you willing to do that, Mom?" I asked. "Are you willing to go into the hospital?"

After I explained and assured her that I would handle the cable guy and pick up her Shih Tzu, Tiny, she relented. All her fight had left her. "OK, if that's what I need to do," was all she said.

She wasn't admitting to any mental illness, but she'd just been booked at the police station. Even she knew everything wasn't OK.

I drove her straight to the hospital without stopping at her apartment or anywhere else. I didn't want to lose any momentum. After finding a hospital with an open bed for her, filling out paperwork, hanging around waiting rooms, and completing all the other tedious steps that grease the wheels of institutionalization, she was admitted that day.

The lobby outside of the psychiatric ward had a set of lockers, and we found a locker for her and put her stuff in it. Then I said goodbye.

"How long am I gonna be here?" Chlotene asked.

The social worker said, "You'll talk about that with the doctor. No longer than you need to be."

"They don't keep people in these places for a long time like they used to," I added. "Probably just a few days."

In the end, it was almost a month.

She had to leave her entire life behind that day. I reassured her I'd be picking up Tiny as soon as I left the hospital. I told her I'd bring her some clothes. I wasn't allowed to bring her anything else, not even books.

"OK, Mom," I said, waving. "I'll be back to visit you. I'll be back as soon as they let me come."

"OK," she said. She seemed to be taking this new development pretty well.

I don't think she knew what was coming. She didn't know how the medication was going to make her feel, or that she would lose one hundred pounds within the following year as a side effect of her schizophrenia medication.

She didn't know the medication would cause such pronounced tremors that another doctor would diagnose her with Parkinson's disease, and she'd take Parkinson's medication unnecessarily for the next twelve months.

She didn't know that her schizophrenia medication would have another bizarre side effect of bleeding her dry of her affection for her dog, Tiny, whom she gave away two months later. She just didn't have it in her to care about Tiny anymore.

She didn't know that while she was still in the hospital, each day of her stay would be scheduled from early in the morning to late at night. She knew she'd have to share a room, but she didn't know she'd witness patients acting out violently. She didn't know that one night she'd wake up in the dark to a shadow of a man standing over, watching her sleep.

"Go back to your bed," she'd have to tell him sternly.

She didn't know that she'd seem pretty sane by comparison to the other patients, as long as you didn't get her talking about her neighbors.

She also didn't know that she wouldn't have access to caffeine, so in addition to beginning a new medication regimen for schizophrenia, she'd also have to deal with headaches from caffeine withdrawal.

She didn't even know how awful the hospital food would be. That it made public school cafeteria food look five-star rated. That it would taste like it was made by people who didn't know they were feeding actual human beings, or didn't care.

She didn't know all that when she waved goodbye.

11

THE DAY the SWAT team confronted me at Chlotene's apartment, stuck fingers in my face, and raced to the psychiatric hospital to arrest her came a few days after I had waved goodbye to Chlotene at the hospital.

That night, just a few hours after the whole SWAT team ordeal, Mark got home from work, and I told him what had happened. The guns like beauty pageant sashes. The deaf building manager and his echoing interpreter.

When I was done with the story, Mark's first concern was whether I would be "after" money to help pay for my mom's defense.

"I'm not paying for this!" he said, ready to engage in an argument. But the argument never came.

I saw the space, the opening into a cavernous well into which I would regularly dive to get him to *see*, to stop attacking and start empathizing, the space where I would feel attacked and appalled and *deeply* offended that he would ever think that I would be after him for money when I had done so much for him. The space into which I would plunge and talk and talk until he would finally, one day, get it.

But instead of diving into that well, I stayed on solid ground. Dry land. I let the space remain but didn't dive into it. It was suddenly obvious to me that all that thrashing around would never change the fact that he had no comfort to offer me.

I couldn't make Mark see anything. I couldn't make him want to stay married to me. I couldn't make him stop hoarding or start acting differently or thinking differently. I started to see I wasn't in charge of fixing him.

That night, I packed my things.

———

These days, it's become more and more common to chirp, "You got this!" at someone whenever they're facing a difficult situation or a struggle.

"You got this!"

It's meant to be a show of support, I guess. But I hate "You got this." I hear in it the dismissal of the entire uncomfortable fact that sometimes we are just in a shitty situation, and once we get there, it sucks, and we don't know if it will change.

My whole life, though, I realized I had been telling myself, "You got this." I could handle whatever came my way, that I had to fix each thing that was wrong in every relationship I was in, and if I couldn't, then I knew I could always cut it out of my life. Abandon it. That's what I'd done over and over again, cutting out relationships when they got too hard or hurt too much.

Looking back now, that night I came home to Mark, our marriage had already been disintegrating for years—for as long as we had been married. I had tried one thing after another. I didn't want to "admit defeat." Much more urgently, I didn't want to be alone.

But that night, I realized I wasn't admitting anything. I was just, for the first time, seeing what was in front of me.

I could not fix my relationship with Mark, and I couldn't make him want to stay married. I emotionally threw my hands up. *I am powerless over this situation, and I can't manage this alone.*

"We admitted we were powerless over alcohol— that our lives had become unmanageable."

That's Step One of Alcoholics Anonymous. Maybe I'd been paying closer attention in the AA meetings than I'd realized because that night something clicked. I had understood for a long time that our marriage was dysfunctional. But when I admitted I didn't have the power to make Mark want to work with me and fix it, that was the moment when I was willing to let go. Cooperate with Mark's request for a divorce.

"Hey, sissy!" my sister Michelle picked up the phone. Growing up, she had always dreamed of having a sister.

"Can I stay in your extra room? Until I get a place of my own? It won't be long."

"Yeah. When do you want to come over?"

She didn't need to think about it. She wanted to be there for her sister.

I started packing immediately.

I let go of Mark and followed a hunch that took several more years to put into words. I took my first step away from an inevitable relapse and toward recovery from alcoholism. I still hadn't admitted I was powerless over alcohol, but I had seen I was powerless over *something*—something I'd been trying to control for a long time.

My relationships, my alcoholism, my watching Chlotene get charged with aggravated arson. They all required me to sit with my intense discomfort over the fact that I didn't know how to fix any of it.

Fix Chlotene? How could I "fix" Chlotene after a lifetime of trying?

Since I'd stopped drinking in 2014, my relationship with my daughters didn't improve, but at least it stopped getting worse. Throughout the worst of my alcoholism, they never cut off contact with me, but they also were understandably wary of me. They didn't proactively reach out because I'd hurt them too many times. But they would meet up with me when invited, and they still spent some of their time with me on holidays.

We started getting lunch together once every month or two. They always made sure that they were both together at every lunch. We kept our conversations superficial. I told them about the latest new website I was working on. They'd catch me up on their lives or the goings-on on their dad's side of the family. We stayed away from anything conflictual.

At first they didn't mention that Chlotene had been calling them, but eventually Barbara told me about the calls a few months before Chlo set the fire.

"Something's wrong with Grandma," she said matter-of-factly.

"Oh, yeah?" I asked. "What's going on?"

"She keeps calling at night. Asking if me or Rachel is there," she said.

"Like, there at her place?" I asked.

"Yeah, like, in her building. She says she can hear us talking with her neighbors."

"What do you tell her?" I asked.

"I tell her I'm at home in bed," she said. "She's been calling a lot. I just quit answering."

"She's been calling me too," I said. "But not that much. She thinks her neighbors are in a gang."

We both laughed at that vision of her elderly neighbors—many of whom needed walkers to get around the building.

So our relationship had been thawing all throughout 2014, and they knew Grandma was acting even more weird than usual.

Soon after Chlotene was discharged from the hospital, I called Barbara because I needed help.

"Hey, you answered the phone!" I said when Barbara answered.

I had just landed a consulting contract that required me to be out of town for a few days. But Chlotene had a court appointment on one of those days.

"Will you take Grandma?" I pleaded. "It's important. She can't get there alone."

"No," Barbara said.

"What's going on?" I asked. "Are you sure?"

"No, I don't know what I have going on."

"What?" I said, shocked. "Why can't you do this for me?"

"I don't want to. Grandma and I are not that close," she said flatly.

"I can't believe you won't do this. This is your *family*," I said, as if I had pulled out an ace in my pocket.

No, she wouldn't drive Grandma there. No, she wouldn't drive Grandma anywhere. No, she wouldn't call Grandma.

I hung up, furious. I made other arrangements for Chlotene that day, but I resented Barbara for saying no to me. How could she do that to me?

Now, I see it differently. I see something that Barbara was showing me, even though she didn't know it. She didn't *have to* help me. She didn't have to help me help Chlotene.

I came to realize that *Barbara is not me.* She was living her own life, making her own choices. I didn't have to understand her or approve of her for her to have her own life or for her choices to be valid.

She was showing me how to be an adult woman who didn't owe her mother anything. Which meant that I didn't *have to* help Chlotene either.

I was helping my own mom because I chose to help her. I wasn't even sure that I wanted to help her. It was a choice, but I hadn't treated it that way. I'd acted as if I had no choice. It was a mindless reflex. As a child, I was the victim of Chlotene's capricious, impulsive, incomprehensible mind. Was I still a victim?

My helping her deal with the consequences of untreated schizophrenia was a choice, and it had been my choice ever since I'd moved out at eighteen years old.

I'd moved out, but I'd still felt responsible for her from the moment in 1988 when I shoved all those boxes into Tim's car until this moment twenty-six years later when Barbara stood up to me.

From then on, I treated my involvement in helping Chlotene as a choice. Even when I sacrificed time and money to get her to court dates and appointments, I reminded myself I was doing it because I wanted to. She wasn't making me. I wasn't doing it because I had to. God knows I wasn't doing it because she deserved the help.

Barbara hadn't given in to the pressure of a sense of obligation that I was forcing on her. I didn't have to give in to that pressure of obligation either.

Barbara helped me realize, too, that it was OK to admit to myself that Chlotene didn't deserve my care. She hadn't earned it. She'd put me through so much my entire life, just by virtue of the fact that I was her daughter. But I chose to show up for her anyway.

Chlotene waved goodbye to me at the hospital the day she checked herself in, not knowing what would happen or whether or not I would really come back.

But I did go back.

I went back almost every day with news about Tiny and about my daughters, and listened to her talk about her "roommates" and the difficult routine she had to follow.

After she was released from the hospital, and every day in the months that followed, I checked in with myself regularly. "Do I want to help Chlotene with this?" I would ask myself.

I kept asking it over the endless weeks of her court hearings. As we emptied our pockets and walked through the metal detector: *Do I want to help Chlotene?* As I would sit with her, waiting for her lawyer and the prosecutor to do their lawyerly dance: *Do I want to help Chlotene?*

Do I want to help Chlotene? I asked myself over and over, for nearly a year, until a plea bargain was finally reached.

Through that year, from the time she set the fire to the time when she finally reached a deal and was put on probation, she became very fragile.

The schizophrenia medication was making her rapidly lose weight. When she left the hospital, the amount of physical space she took up shrank, and not just because of the weight loss. Before the fire, she used a bulky walker with a built-in seat and a basket. She would put Tiny in the basket and tour around her building. But after she got out of the hospital, she stopped using the walker. She took up as little space as she could with her body.

Her movement and her thinking slowed considerably. She couldn't remember how to do simple things that she'd previously had no trouble with. At first, I found this frustrating. I wasn't ready for this new dullness. Whatever else she'd been, she'd always been sharp. She'd always been a learner. But now it felt like she wasn't trying—like she wasn't willing to engage. I got her a cell phone, and it took her ages to learn how to use it to make outgoing calls. Of course, that might be typical of some older adults, but it hadn't been typical of Chlotene before the hospitalization.

I took her to the grocery store, and on the walk from the parking lot to the front door, she hooked her arm into mine as though she needed that support. That was also new.

She seemed all-around older than her seventy-four years, simultaneously more frightened and more detached.

And even with this new fragility, I knew I had to enforce limits and boundaries that it had never before occurred to me to enforce.

I was not willing to go broke to pay for her defense. I was not going to take her to appointments that I simply couldn't get to, even if that meant she might miss one or two.

I knew that meant I might have to watch her go to prison and die in prison.

Maybe that sounds dramatic. But for many months, her case felt almost intolerably uncertain. "What's gonna happen?"

After the visit from the SWAT team, I couldn't write off her fear of prison as coming from her paranoia and nowhere else. The possibility of her having to serve time was real.

The day after the SWAT team came, I called the detective that handled Chlotene's case. He explained to me that the district attorney's office was charging her with a first-degree felony. First degree, as in, murder, rape, and . . . aggravated arson. He told me that the day after I'd brought Chlotene in for booking, he'd had a meeting with the county prosecutor who had "ripped him a new asshole" for not taking Chlotene into custody right away. He claimed the County Prosecutor then insisted on a first-degree felony charge, based on the report.

"Felony One means immediate arrest," he explained. "If you're not in jail already, we come get you."

I started to realize just how much trouble Chlotene was in. If she was convicted, she faced major prison time. As a fragile seventy-four-year-old, she would die in prison.

She'd set fire to someone else's residence in a senior housing community. It felt infinitely empty to say something like, "Don't worry, Mom, it'll be fine," and pat her on the back the way I did all those years ago in Phoenix when her money was stolen from her purse. Or when she "saw" my biological dad drive by in his white Cadillac when I was fifteen. Or when she rushed over to our house in a cab to find me and make sure I was all right and Mark answered the door.

My reassurance calmed her down, but it didn't fix anything.

For the first time, just like I'd realized with Mark, I realized with Chlotene that *I didn't know if everything was going to be OK.*

She ended up staying at the hospital for almost a month before being discharged. The SWAT team visit to the hospital made the staff extra vigilant, and they didn't want to let her go until they were sure they could detect no signs of violence.

She had so many appointments once the hospital discharged her. Court dates, psychiatric appointments, evaluations, community mental health, doctor's appointments. So much to do, yet whatever I *could* do, I could not prevent Chlotene from going to prison. I had a few thousand dollars to spend on her defense, but that was it.

If a prosecutor wanted her to go to jail to await trial, or to get convicted, even die in prison, I couldn't do anything about that. She had, after all, set the fire. She didn't have innocence on her side. What she did have on her side was her little-old-lady innocent demeanor. But would that be enough?

Just as it had with Mark, my brain flashed the thought, *What if I just stopped?*

What if I just stopped trying to fix it, to contain it, to make it so Chlotene was OK? She wasn't OK. The doctors were telling me that. Her arrest was telling me that.

My daughter Barbara was telling me that. She wouldn't be involved in fixing and patching up and holding things together.

Maybe I shouldn't try to do that either. Maybe I couldn't even if I wanted to.

I don't got this.

12

Are you going to a meeting tonight? It was a text from Kathy.
I'm going to the Fellowship Hall meeting. You? I responded.
See you there, she texted back.

I had been going to meetings almost daily for a couple of months. I liked Kathy. She was young and smart. A woman with her own business. She hung around the edges of AA like me. We didn't cross paths often, but I liked talking with her after meetings when I had the chance. I related to her, and she seemed so "put together." But she was having a hard time staying sober.

She walked into the meeting late and sat behind me.

After the meeting, we stood near the back of the room at the refreshment table. We stared while a man with stained clothes and visibly dirty hands touched every single cookie on the tray before finally selecting one.

"Want a cookie?" I asked, turning to her.

"Oh my God," she laughed. "Sometimes I wonder if I belong here."

"Me too," I said.

"Then why do you come back?" she asked.

I looked down and paused. "I don't know of any other way that works." I pointed over my shoulder toward a group of women chatting near the front of the room. "They've got it figured out," I said.

With perfect timing, the women burst out into laughter over something. These were women who wholeheartedly embraced the AA way of life. They had become familiar faces. They welcomed me.

"I want what they have," I said.

Kathy looked surprised at my response.

"They seem happy," I said.

I didn't have to figure anything out or wonder how I was going to make my life better. All I had to do was show up to meetings and start working the twelve steps with a sponsor.

So that's what I did. I decided to put recovery from alcoholism at the center of my life, and the program that AA offered was the only way I knew how to do that.

If I had written a letter to myself at the end of 2014 and filled it with all the things I hoped my life would be like in five years, it would have been short. I didn't hope for much.

It would have said something like . . .

Dear Emily,

I hope you're doing OK. I hope you are happy and don't think about alcohol during all your waking hours.

I hope your life is back to the way it was before alcohol had this death grip on your mind.

I hope you're able to get something like your old life back.

I had no idea what was possible for me or even what I wanted. And, in order to find out, I had to move forward, doing and having things that I couldn't even imagine. I had to listen to those women who already had what I wanted and let them help me through the twelve steps.

I never got my old life back.

I sat across from my daughter Rachel on the outdoor patio of a local restaurant. We had ordered the same thing, and she was digging into her Thai burrito. It was sunny, but the tables and chairs were wet.

I was talking more than I was eating.

Rachel listened while I cataloged and owned up to the poor decisions I had made prior to recovery.

I was wrong when . . .

I hurt you and didn't think about your feelings when . . .

I should have been there for you when . . .

"Is there anything I can do to make up for what I did?" I asked.

The wounds were no longer fresh. Over the past few years, my daughters had seen me change as a result of recovery. Our relationships had improved. They had finished college. I had become reliable and capable of supporting myself financially. I had my own apartment.

Rachel paused to consider my question and then shrugged her shoulders. "You're doing good," Rachel said with a smile. "Just keep doing what you're doing."

The following week, I had a similar conversation with my daughter Barbara.

"OK, we're good," she said in response to the same question I had asked Rachel.

It wasn't quite the response I had expected. But what was I expecting? Forgiveness?

I knew that was too much to ask.

Instead, I wanted something more meaningful that would take more time. I wanted their respect. I had never sought their respect before I started recovery. Before then, I had always wanted their compliance. I had wanted them to listen to me because they felt an obligation to do so. Now, I wanted to earn their trust. That was harder.

Barbara leaned back into the patio chair and asked, "How long do you have to keep going to those meetings?"

"It's good for me to just keep going back," I said.

13

"Oh, no. I'm sorry. I haven't time to play any longer," said Pippi. "But it was fun."

Then she took hold of the policemen by their belts and carried them down the garden path, out through the gate, and onto the street.

. . .

And the policemen hurried back to the town and told all the ladies and gentlemen that Pippi wasn't quite fit for a children's home. (They didn't tell that they had been up on the roof.) And the ladies and gentlemen decided that it would be best after all to let Pippi remain in villa Villekulla, and if she wanted to go to school, she could make the arrangements herself.[1]

I WAS TALKING to my half-sister Michelle on Zoom in September 2020, and she said to me, "I really think Chlotene's living her best life now. Her conviction ended up being the best thing that happened to her. She didn't have to pay court costs or a fine. But she had to continue going to a schizophrenia support group, to meet with her probation officer, to continue to seek treatment with a psychiatrist . . . It seemed like everything the court had ordered her to do was good for her."

Best. Life.

"Why couldn't she have done something stupid like that a while ago?" Michelle asked wistfully.

"Well, she did," I said, careful to keep any edge out of my voice. "She did do stupid things." I recalled how Chlotene drove unregistered cars in Phoenix. How we lived with strangers. How many times I climbed onto our apartment building roof or sat in strangers' cars without any adult to stop me.

"She was a woman," I said carefully. "Having me with her as a young child in some ways protected her. Plus, if she didn't have a child, she probably wouldn't have been at all invested in keeping herself safe at all."

It's hard to give Chlotene credit for anything, but the truth is she was not completely oblivious. "She at least knew she couldn't leave me home alone as a toddler, that I had to go to school," I said, recalling one of the families she'd left me with whose sons regularly beat me up. "I think she was able to get compassion from people because she was a mom," I concluded uneasily.

Is she "living her best life" now?

I think so. But just like when someone's "best" isn't good enough, sometimes their "best life" isn't really a very good one.

In so many of the Pippi Longstocking stories, as hard as she might try to be good, Pippi always ended up in trouble. Except Pippi was a girl and a fiction. Chlotene was a seventy-four-year-old woman when she set the fire in her senior apartment complex.

She is lucky she found treatment. She is lucky to be stable. And she's lucky to be alive.

But before she received treatment, Chlo was charming and full of interest in life. She followed the news, astrology. She read tarot cards. She had Tiny.

> Hi Em,
>
> Hope you are done with the Indy travel, etc. I was really worried about you and your driving in all of this heavy rain we had these last two days.
>
> Wednesday, I took a cab to SBH medical and got Tiny's liquid medication. She takes it twice a day, and her heart medication once a day.
>
> Nothing happening here. I did hear on the news that you can double your money: By folding it over and putting it in your pocket. Ha Ha.
>
> Love, Mom and Tiny

When she started her medication for schizophrenia, she had major side effects. She developed a flat affect. Talking to her suddenly became uncomfortably boring. She was monosyllabic. Her lack of interest in conversation made me realize that a lot of what had fueled her conversations in the past were her delusions. We never had normal conversations, and now that she didn't have delusions anymore, there was little to say, even after her doctor found a better medication.

She didn't care about tarot or astrology anymore either. She always retained the flat affect. She would just lose interest on the phone after about ten minutes.

Her charm seemed to be tightly interwoven with her paranoid delusions, and the medication caused her to lose both. When I look back at her emails from before the fire, I can see that.

Hi Em,

. . . At Sugar grove now, they use the two entrances that were created for people to go over to Walmart as a racetrack all night long now. Just going around in circles. Plus I know the ways of these people here, and know who to avoid.

Hi Em,

. . . Other Shih Tzu here named Franny has what looks like dandruff. Owner, Julie, says doctor thinks dog has allergies and should have a spoon of olive oil each day, but that was a week ago, and the dandruff stuff has doubled. Looks to me like they have been washing her with human instead of dog shampoo.

[Online], found a house for $500 down, total cost 13,500 at $99 per month. I would definately [sic] consider that if it is in Franklin County, so I would still have cab service.

From 2012:

Good morning relatives, friends and acquaintances,

This is a letter letting you know of the Tarot readings that I do for myself and others.

I want you to know that I can always do a Tarot reading for you over the phone, or thru a question you send me in the mail. You would ideally call me at least an hour before the reading, and let me know what your question for the Tarot is.

Then, I could do all of the research in my various card decks and give you a much better reading than [an] on the spot reading can do. Your birth date would be helpful, but not necessary.

I want to make it clear that there is no monetary charge, I am simply [an] old lady trying to reach out to people with an old science that I have discovered. It has worked for me and often takes the burden of decision much lighter.

Living her best life now.

She's certainly living a more stable life than she ever has. Recently during one of our weekly phone conversations, she told me a new next-door neighbor had moved in with a dog, and the dog wouldn't stop barking. She seemed annoyed; I even glimpsed an ember of anger glinting from underneath her flat tone of voice.

So I responded by saying, "You know what? If that dog is bothering you, then he's bothering other neighbors too. I'm sure one of them will say something about it. Let's just see how it goes. Maybe the dog is just getting used to his new apartment."

She agreed. The next week, I checked in.

"The dog's fine," she said. "I think he was just getting used to the place."

Fantastic, I thought. That meant her annoyance with the dog wasn't a symptom of anything else.

But I can never assume that. A part of me will always worry she will lie to me about taking her medication and develop new, unspoken delusions about her neighbors and burn the entire building down before I realize what's happening. I've seen too much to fool myself into anything else.

She has the choice to stop the meds, decompensate, and become psychotic, unable to do the things she needed to do to stay on her own. Then she would do something that could land her in jail, hurt someone, hurt herself.

Or she can choose to live a life on medication that deadens her interest in the world but keeps her and the people around her much more safe.

Even though it's been years, I still regularly ask her directly if she's taking her medication for her schizophrenia. "Are you still taking your schizophrenia medicine?"

That's how I phrase it.

She'd prefer I call it "her nervous pills." But I won't. One of the things that she needs to do in order to stay safe and preempt any delusions is take her medication.

But another thing she needs to do to keep taking her medication is be as honest with herself as she can that she has schizophrenia. She needs to be reminded. I need to remind her. Schizophrenics Anonymous reminds her.

I *need* to use the phrase "your schizophrenia medication." If I called them her "nervous pills," I'd be minimizing her illness. And I'd be protecting her feelings because she would love to pretend she doesn't have a severe mental illness. But pretending she doesn't have a severe mental illness in order to spare her feelings puts her in danger.

As I learned to remind her directly that she has an illness, I realized the same is true of my alcoholism. To be an active alcoholic is to live inside a delusion.

I lived inside a delusion. I believed that I was not an alcoholic and that things weren't that bad. I had a rationale for every terrible decision I made. I justified my behavior by minimizing it, by deflecting any questions about it. By gaslighting those around me.

You'd drink too if you were married to my husband.

Or, *Can't you see I'm dealing with constant back pain? All I want to do is not live in pain.*

Part of the treatment for alcoholism involves not minimizing how bad it was.

Did that really happen?
Was it really that bad?
Did it even matter?

Yes, during my Senate campaign, I had a drunk volunteer driving me around.

That really did happen. It really was that bad. It really did matter.

Yes, I gave up custody of my youngest daughter willingly during her senior year in high school. I chose drinking over her.

That really did happen. It really was that bad. It really did matter.

Yes, I married two men I didn't love within three years.

That really did happen. It really was that bad. It really did matter.

A very large part of my recovery from alcoholism is the daily maintenance of my tether to reality. I guess you could call that honest thinking.

If I couldn't be honest with myself, then how could I be honest with others? I learned how to be honest in the rooms of AA. I don't try to forget or deny the past. My past actions —what I did and who it hurt—remind me that alcoholism is a mental illness. It wasn't a stage. I wasn't just "nervous." I wasn't *just* weak-minded. **I was in the delusion of alcoholic denial. It was *that* bad.**

Chlotene and I, after all our screw-ups and let downs and failures and nearly-much-worse moments, both lucked into responding to the treatments we tried.

Just as my mom will always need to receive treatment for schizophrenia, there's no return to drinking "normally" for me. "Once you're a pickle, you can't go back to being a cucumber."

So I continue to take things one day at a time.

———

I bought Chlotene a Mac computer so she could have reliable access to the internet and the outside world. She called to tell me she couldn't get the computer to work no matter what she did. The display was on, but nothing happened when she tried to use it.

I told her I'd be by to take a look. When I got there, I futzed with the computer a bit. I picked up the keyboard and noticed she'd found the small on/off switch and turned it off.

"Oh, hey, Mom, this is the problem. Just leave this switch on. You don't need to worry about burning out the battery," I chuckled.

A moment later, someone knocked on the door. Chlotene got up to open it. It was a friend coming to take her to church, one of the very few places she ventures to regularly.

"Take your time here, Emily," she said as she was leaving.

"OK," I said. "I don't have a key, though."

"A key?" she asked.

"Yeah, to lock the door when I leave."

"Oh," she said. "Well, don't worry about locking it up. No one's gonna come in here."

And she left.

NOTES

Epigraph

1. Astrid Lindgren, *Pippi Longstocking* (New York: Puffin Books, 1997), 117.

Part I

1. Astrid Lindgren, *Pippi Longstocking* (New York: Puffin Books, 1997), 95.

Chapter 1

1. Astrid Lindgren, *Pippi Longstocking* (New York: Puffin Books, 1997), 116–117.
2. American Psychiatric Association, *Diagnostic and Statistical Manual of Mental Disorders*, 4th ed. (Washington, DC: American Psychiatric Publishing, Inc., 1994), 276.

Chapter 3

1. Special Supplemental Nutrition Program for Women, Infants, and Children.

Part II

1. Astrid Lindgren, *Pippi Longstocking* (New York: Puffin Books, 1997), 117.

Chapter 5

1. American Psychiatric Association, *Diagnostic and Statistical Manual of Mental Disorders*, 4th ed. (Washington DC: American Psychiatric Publishing, Inc., 1994), 276.

Chapter 6

1. American Psychiatric Association, *Diagnostic and Statistical Manual of Mental Disorders*, 4th ed. (Washington, DC: American Psychiatric Publishing, Inc., 1994), 284.
2. Ibid., 285.
3. Ibid., 287.
4. American Psychiatric Association, *Diagnostic and Statistical Manual of Mental Disorders*, 4th ed. (Washington, DC: American Psychiatric Publishing, Inc., 1994), 285.

Chapter 7

1. John Reed, "John T. Reed's analysis of Robert T. Kiyosaki's book Rich Dad, Poor Dad, Part 1," *John T. Reed*, September 3, 2015, https://johntreed.com/blogs/john-t-reed-s-real-estate-investment-blog/61651011-john-t-reeds-analysis-of-robert-t-kiyosakis-book-rich-dad-poor-dad-part-1.
2. Ramit Sethi, "Book Review: Rich Dad, Poor Dad (this book irks me)," *I Will Teach You to Be Rich*, March 31, 2006, https://www.iwillteachyoutoberich.com/blog/book-review-rich-dad-poor-dad-this-books-irks-me/.

Chapter 13

1. Astrid Lindgren, *Pippi Longstocking* (New York: Puffin Books, 1997), 46.

ACKNOWLEDGEMENTS

Thank you Maggie Frank-Hsu for your commitment and unflagging enthusiasm for this project. This book would not have been written without your artful mastery of the writing process.

To Adam Knolls for witnessing my process, reflecting with me, and making space for my voice. You are in this book even though you are not in this book.

To Michelle Neubauer for showing up for me without fail like the sister I had always wished for.

To Roy and Eloise Tefertiller for saying yes and accepting me as family.

To librarians for introducing me to new worlds and bringing me hope for my future.

To Fred Rogers for singing and talking to me when I was lonely.

To the cast of Sesame Street 1973 to 1978 for singing with me and showing me examples of support and friendship.

To my friends for helping me understand what it means to be a friend by example.

Everyone who has been my family past and present.

ABOUT THE AUTHOR

Emily Journey is a writer, speaker, and instructor. She is the founder and CEO of Emily Journey & Associates, a digital consulting agency that serves companies throughout the United States and internationally. She lives in Columbus, Ohio with her husband Adam, where she enjoys walking in her neighborhood, chatting with the neighbors, and spending time with her daughters and sons-in-law.

Visit https://idontgotthisbook.com for author notes and bonus content for readers.

www.ingramcontent.com/pod-product-compliance
Lightning Source LLC
Chambersburg PA
CBHW020907080526
44589CB00011B/472